BASIC
ENGLISH GRAMMAR
Second Edition

Volume B

Betty Schrampfer Azar

PRENTICE HALL REGENTS

Upper Saddle River, New Jersey 07458

Library of Congress Cataloging-in-Publication Data

Azar, Betty Scrampfer, 1941-
   Basic English grammar / Betty Schrampfer Azar. -- 2nd ed.
     p.   cm.
   Includes indexes.
   ISBN 0-13-368424-5 (v. 1). -- ISBN 0-13-368358-3 (v. 2)
   1. English language--Textbooks for foreign speakers. 2. English
language--Grammar--Problems, exercises, etc.   I. Title.
PE1128.A96   1995
428.2'4--dc20
                                            92-25711
                                             CIP

Publisher: *Tina B. Carver*
Director of Production and Manufacturing: *Aliza Greenblatt*
Editorial Production/Design Manager: *Dominick Mosco*
Editorial/Production Supervision: *Janet Johnston*
Editorial Assistant: *Shelley Hartle*
Production Coordinator: *Ray Keating*
Cover Coordinator: *Merle Krumper*
Cover Production: *Molly Pike Riccardi*
Cover Design: *Joel Mitnick Design*
Interior Design: *Ros Herion Freese*
Illustrations: *Don Martinetti*

©1996 by Betty Schrampfer Azar

Published by PRENTICE HALL REGENTS
Prentice-Hall, Inc.
A Simon & Schuster Company
Upper Saddle River, New Jersey 07458

Printed in the United States of America.

10 9 8 7 6 5 4 3

ISBN 0-13-368358-3

Prentice-Hall International (UK) Limited, *London*
Prentice-Hall of Australia Pty., Limited, *Sydney*
Prentice-Hall Canada Inc., *Toronto*
Prentice-Hall Hispanoamericana, S.A., *Mexico*
Prentice-Hall of India Private Limited, *New Delhi*
Prentice-Hall of Japan, Inc., *Tokyo*
Simon & Schuster Asia Pte. Ltd., *Singapore*
Editora Prentice-Hall do Brasil, Ltda., *Rio de Janeiro*

Contents

Chapter 10 EXPRESSING IDEAS WITH VERBS

Preface to the Second Edition

Basic English Grammar remains a developmental skills text for students of English as a second or foreign language. Serving as both a reference and a workbook, it introduces students to the form, meaning, and usage of basic structures in English. It provides ample opportunities for practice through extensive and varied exercises leading to communicative activities. Although it focuses on grammar, it promotes the development of all language skills.

This second edition has a greatly expanded range of contents to provide a solid core of basic English grammar for lower-level or beginning students. It includes numerous new exercises with, at the end of each chapter, cumulative review exercises that include additional communicative and interactive student-centered tasks.

Also available are an *Answer Key*, with answers only, and a *Teacher's Guide*, with teaching suggestions as well as the answers to the exercises.

Acknowledgments

Writing English grammar texts is a pleasure for me. In this pursuit, I am helped by many wonderful people: dedicated teachers who give presentations at conferences and write articles for regional newsletters or international journals; researchers who explore the hows and whys of second language acquisition; grammarians who present their observations clearly and convincingly; past and present authors of other ESL/EFL grammar materials who show creative and sound approaches to helping students gain understanding and usage ability of English; colleagues who give me valuable feedback and share their pedagogical insights; and publishing professionals who know how to mold and market educational materials. We all rely on one another.

Above all, I am indebted to my students, who have taught me a great deal about the language acquisition process by openly sharing with me their learning experiences and practical needs.

In sum, I am indebted to the ESL/EFL community of teachers, researchers, authors, publishers, and students.

In particular, I thank Tina Carver, Janet Johnston, and Shelley Hartle for their invaluable professionalism as well as friendship. I also wish to thank Barbara Matthies, Irene Juzkiw, Stacy Hagen, Nancy Price, Lawrence Cisar, Don Martinetti, Lizette Reyes, Stella Reilly, Marita Froimson, Joy Edwards, R.T. Steltz, Sue Van Etten, Ken Kortlever, Generessa Arielle, and Chelsea Azar. My gratitude goes also to the many wonderful teachers and publishers I met in Korea, Japan, and Taiwan on my trip to Asia in 1994.

CHAPTER 6

Expressing Future Time

6-1 FUTURE TIME: USING *BE GOING TO*

(a)	I **am going to go** downtown tomorrow.	*Be going to* expresses (talks about) the future.
(b)	Sue **is going to be** here tomorrow afternoon.	
(c)	We **are going to come** to class tomorrow morning.	

FORM:
$$\left. \begin{array}{l} \textbf{\textit{am}} \\ \textbf{\textit{is}} \\ \textbf{\textit{are}} \end{array} \right\} + \textbf{\textit{going}} + \textit{infinitive}\star$$

(d) I**'m not going to go** downtown tomorrow.	NEGATIVE: *be* + *not* + *going to*
(e) Ann **isn't going to study** tonight.	

(f) "**Are** you **going to come** to class tomorrow?" "No, I'm not."	QUESTION: *be* + *subject* + *going to*
(g) "**Is** Jim **going to be** at the meeting tomorrow?" "Yes, he is."	A form of *be* is used in the short answer to a yes/no question with *be going to*, as in (f) and (g). (See Chart 1-9 for information about short answers with *be*.)
(h) "What time **are** you **going to eat** dinner tonight?" "Around six."	

*Infinitive = *to* + the simple form of a verb (*to come, to go, to see, to study,* etc.).

■ **EXERCISE 1—ORAL:** Some activities are listed on the next page. Which of these activities are you going to do tomorrow? Which ones are you not going to do tomorrow? Pair up with a classmate.

STUDENT A: Your book is open. Ask a question. Use *"Are you going to . . . tomorrow?"*

STUDENT B: Your book is closed. Answer the question. Give both a short answer and a long answer. Use *"I'm going to . . . tomorrow"* or *"I'm not going to . . . tomorrow"* in the long answer.

Example: go downtown
STUDENT A: Are you going to go downtown tomorrow?
STUDENT B: Yes, I am. I'm going to go downtown tomorrow. OR:
            No, I'm not. I'm not going to go downtown tomorrow.

Switch roles.

1. get up before eight o'clock
2. come to class
3. stay home all day
4. eat lunch
5. eat lunch with *(someone)*
6. get a haircut
7. watch TV in the evening
8. do something interesting in the evening
9. go to bed early
10. go to bed late

11. get up early
12. get up late
13. walk to school
14. study grammar
15. get some physical exercise
16. eat dinner
17. eat dinner alone
18. listen to music after dinner
19. go shopping
20. do something interesting and unusual

■ **EXERCISE 2—ORAL (BOOKS CLOSED):** Answer the questions.

Example: tomorrow?
TO STUDENT A: What are you going to do tomorrow?
   STUDENT A: I'm going to (go shopping).
TO STUDENT B: What is (. . .) going to do tomorrow?
   STUDENT B: He's/She's going to go shopping.

What are you going to do:

1. tomorrow?
2. tomorrow morning?
3. tomorrow afternoon?
4. tomorrow night?
5. at 7:00 tomorrow morning?

6. at 9:00 tomorrow morning?
7. at noon tomorrow?
8. at 5:00 tomorrow afternoon?
9. around 6:30 tomorrow evening?
10. after 8:00 tomorrow night?

■ **EXERCISE 3:** Complete the sentences. Use **be going to** + the following expressions (or your own words).

call the landlord	✔ *go to the bookstore*	*see a dentist*
call the police	*go to an Italian restaurant*	*stay in bed today*
get something to eat	*lie down and rest for a while*	*take a long walk in the park*
go to the beach	*look it up in my dictionary*	*take it to the post office*
go to bed	*major in psychology*	*take them to the laundromat*

1. I need to buy a book. I _____*am going to go to the bookstore*_____.

2. It's midnight now. I'm sleepy. I _____.

3. Sue is hungry. She _____.

4. My clothes are dirty. I _____.

5. I have a toothache. My wisdom tooth hurts. I _____.

6. I'm writing a composition. I don't know how to spell a word. I _____

_____.

7. George has to mail a package. He _____.

8. Rosa lives in an apartment. There's a problem with the plumbing. She _____

_____.

9. Sue and I want to go swimming. We _____.

10. I have a headache. I _____.

11. It's late at night. I hear a burglar! I _____.

12. I want to be a psychologist. When I go to the university, I _____

_____.

13. I feel terrible. I think I'm getting the flu. I _____.

14. Ivan and Natasha want to go out to eat. They _____.

15. It's a nice day today. Mary and I _____.

■ **EXERCISE 4—ORAL (BOOKS CLOSED):** Listen to the common activities that are described. Picture these activities in your mind. Use *be going to* to tell what you think your classmates are going to do.

Example: (. . .) is carrying his/her textbooks and notebooks. He/She is walking toward the library. What is (. . .) going to do?

Response: (. . .) is going to study at the library.

1. (. . .) is standing next to the chalkboard. He/She is picking up a piece of chalk. What is (. . .) going to do?
2. (. . .) has some letters in his/her hand. He/She is walking toward the post office. What is (. . .) going to do?
3. (. . .) is standing by a telephone. He/She is looking in the telephone book for (. . .)'s name. What is (. . .) going to do?
4. (. . .) put some water on the stove to boil. She got a cup and saucer out of the cupboard and some tea. What is (. . .) going to do?
5. (. . .) is putting on his/her coat. He/She is walking toward the door. What is (. . .) going to do?
6. (. . .) has a basket full of dirty clothes. He/She is walking toward a laundromat. What is (. . .) going to do?
7. (. . .) bought some meat and vegetables at the market. He/She is holding a bag of rice. He/She just turned on the stove. What is (. . .) going to do?
8. (. . .) and (. . .) are walking into *(name of a local restaurant)*. It's seven o'clock in the evening. What are (. . .) and (. . .) going to do?
9. (. . .) gave (. . .) a diamond engagement ring. What are (. . .) and (. . .) going to do?
10. (. . .) and (. . .) have airplane tickets. They're putting clothes in their suitcases. Their clothes include swimming suits and sandals. What are (. . .) and (. . .) going to do?

■ **EXERCISE 5—ORAL:** Ask a classmate a question. Use *be going to*.

Example: when / go downtown
STUDENT A: When are you going to go downtown?
STUDENT B: Tomorrow afternoon. / In a couple of days. / I don't know. / etc.

1. where / go after class today
2. what time / get home tonight
3. when / eat dinner
4. where / eat dinner
5. what time / go to bed tonight
6. what time / get up tomorrow morning
7. where / be tomorrow morning
8. when / see your family again
9. where / live next year
10. when / get married

■ **EXERCISE 6—ORAL:** Answer the questions. Use ***be going to***.

Example: You want to buy some tea. What are you going to do? What is (. . .) going to do and why?

To STUDENT A: You want to buy some tea. What are you going to do?

STUDENT A: I'm going to go to the grocery store.

To STUDENT B: What is (Student A) going to do and why?

STUDENT B: He/She's going to go to the grocery store because he/she wants to buy some tea.

1. You have a toothache. What are you going to do? What is (. . .) going to do and why?
2. You need to mail a package. Where are you going to go? Where is (. . .) going to go and why?
3. Your clothes are dirty.
4. It's midnight. You're sleepy.
5. It's late at night. You hear a burglar.
6. You need to buy some groceries.

7. You want to go swimming.
8. You want to go fishing.
9. You want to buy a new coat.
10. You're hungry.
11. You have a headache.
12. It's a nice day today.
13. You need to cash a check.
14. You want some *(pizza)* for dinner.
15. You're reading a book. You don't know the meaning of a word.

6-2   WORDS USED FOR PAST TIME AND FUTURE TIME

PAST	FUTURE	
yesterday	*tomorrow*	PAST: It *rained* **yesterday**. FUTURE: It's *going to rain* **tomorrow.**
yesterday morning *yesterday afternoon* *yesterday evening* *last night*	*tomorrow morning* *tomorrow afternoon* *tomorrow evening* *tomorrow night*	PAST: I *was* in class **yesterday morning**. FUTURE: I'm *going to be* in class **tomorrow morning.**
last week *last month* *last year* *last weekend* *last spring* *last summer* *last fall* *last winter* *last Monday, etc.*	*next week* *next month* *next year* *next weekend* *next spring* *next summer* *next fall* *next winter* *next Monday, etc.*	PAST: Mary *went* downtown **last week**. FUTURE: Mary *is going to go* downtown **next week.** PAST: Bob *graduated* from high school **last spring**. FUTURE: Ann *is going to graduate* from high school **next spring.**
. . . minutes ago *. . . hours ago* *. . . days ago* *. . . weeks ago* *. . . months ago* *. . . years ago*	*in . . . minutes (from now)* *in . . . hours (from now)* *in . . . days (from now)* *in . . . weeks (from now)* *in . . . months (from now)* *in . . . years (from now)*	PAST: I *finished* my homework **five minutes ago**. FUTURE: Pablo *is going to finish* his homework **in five minutes.**

■ **EXERCISE 7:** Complete the sentences. Use *yesterday*, *last*, *tomorrow*, or *next*.

1. I went swimming ____*yesterday*____ morning.

2. Ken is going to go to the beach ____*tomorrow*____ morning.

3. I'm going to take a trip _____ week.

4. Alice went to Miami _____ week for a short vacation.

5. We had a test in class _____ afternoon.

6. _____ afternoon we're going to go on a picnic.

7. My sister is going to arrive _____ Tuesday.

8. Sam bought a used car _____ Friday.

9. My brother is going to enter the university _____ fall.

10. _____ spring I took a trip to San Francisco.

11. Ann is going to fly to London _____ month.

12. Rick lived in Tokyo _____ year.

13. I'm going to study at the library _____ night.

14. _____ night I watched TV.

15. _____ evening I'm going to go to a baseball game.

16. Matt was at the laundromat _____ evening.

■ **EXERCISE 8:** Complete the sentences. Use the given time expression with *ago* or *in*.

1. *ten minutes*   Class is going to end _____*in ten minutes.*_____

2. *ten minutes*   Ann's class ended _____*ten minutes ago.*_____

3. *an hour*   The post office isn't open. It closed _____

4. *an hour*   Jack is going to call us _____

5. *two more months*   I'm studying abroad now, but I'm going to be back home

   _____

6. *two months*   My wife and I took a trip to Morocco _____

7. *a minute*   Karen left _____

8. *half an hour*   I'm going to meet David at the coffee shop _____

9. *one more week*   The new highway is going to open _____

10. *a year*   I was living in Korea _____

■ **EXERCISE 9:** Complete the sentences. Use *yesterday*, *last*, *tomorrow*, *next*, *in*, or *ago*.

1. I went to the zoo _____*last*_____ week.

2. Yolanda went to the zoo a week _____.

3. Peter Nelson is going to go to the zoo _____ Saturday.

4. We're going to go to the zoo _____ two more days.

5. My children went to the zoo _____ morning.

6. My cousin is going to go to the zoo _____ afternoon.

7. Kim Yang-Don graduated from Sogang University _____ spring.

8. I'm going to take a vacation in Canada _____ summer.

9. We're going to have company for dinner _____ night.

10. We had company for dinner three days _____.

11. We're going to have dinner at our friends' house _____ two days.

12. _____ evening we're going to go to a concert.

13. _____ Friday I went to a party.

14. _____ morning the students took a test.

15. I took a test two days _____.

16. The students are going to have another test _____ Thursday.

17. Are you going to be home _____ afternoon around three?

18. My little sister arrived here _____ month.

19. She is going to leave _____ two weeks.

20. _____ year Yuko is going to be a freshman in college.

6-3 USING *A COUPLE OF* OR *A FEW* WITH *AGO* (PAST) AND *IN* (FUTURE)

(a) Sam arrived here **one** (OR: **a**) *year ago.* (b) Jack is going to be here *in* **two** *minutes.* (c) I talked to Ann **three** *days ago.*	Numbers are often used in time expressions with **ago** and **in**.
(d) I saw Carlos **a couple of** *months ago.* (e) He's going to return to Mexico in **a couple of** *months.* (f) I got a letter from Gina **a few** *weeks ago.* (g) I got a letter to see Gina in **a few** *weeks.*	**A couple of** and **a few** are also commonly used. **A couple of** means "two." *A couple of months ago* = two months ago. **A few** means "a small number, not a large number." *A few weeks ago* = three, four, or five weeks ago.
(h) I began college last year. I'm going to graduate *in* **two more** *years.* My sister is almost finished with her education. She's going to graduate *in* **a few more** *months.* She's going to graduate *in* **three more** *months.*	Frequently the word **more** is used in future time expressions that begin with **in**.

■ **EXERCISE 10:** Complete the sentences, using information from your own life. Use the words in *italics*. Use **ago** or **in**. Use numbers (*one, two, three, ten, sixteen,* etc.) or the expressions **a couple of** or **a few**.

1. *days*   We studied Chapter 5 <u>*a couple of days ago/three days ago/etc.*</u>

2. *days*   We're going to finish this chapter <u>*in a few more days /*</u>
    <u>*in three or four days / etc.*</u>

3. *hours*   I ate breakfast _____

4. *hours*   I'm going to eat lunch/dinner _____

5. *minutes* We finished Exercise 9 _____

6. *minutes* This class is going to end _____

7. *years* I was born _____

8. *years* My parents got married _____

9. *years* I got/am going to get married _____

10. *weeks*
    months   I arrived in this city _____, and I'm
    years

    going to leave this city _____

■ **EXERCISE 11:** Complete the sentences. Use your own words. Write about your life. For example, what did you do a few days ago? What are you going to do in a few days?

1. _____ a few days ago.

2. _____ in a few days *(from now)*.

3. _____ in a few more minutes.

4. _____ three hours ago.

5. _____ in four more hours.

6. _____ a couple of days ago.

7. _____ in a couple of months *(from now)*.

8. _____ a few minutes ago.

9. _____ many years ago.

10. _____ in a couple of minutes *(from now)*.

6-4 USING *TODAY, TONIGHT,* AND *THIS* + *MORNING, AFTERNOON, EVENING, WEEK, MONTH, YEAR*

PRESENT	Right now it's 10 A.M. We are in our English class. (a) We **are studying** English **this morning**.	*today* *tonight* *this morning* *this afternoon* *this evening* *this week* *this weekend* *this month* *this year*	These words can express present, past, or future time.
PAST	Right now it's 10 A.M. Nancy left home at 9 A.M. to go downtown. She isn't at home right now. (b) Nancy **went** downtown **this morning**.		
FUTURE	Right now it's 10 A.M. Class ends at 11 A.M. After class today, I'm going to go to the post office. (c) I**'m going to go** to the post office **this morning**.		

■ **EXERCISE 12:**   Answer the questions. Use your own words.

1. What is something you did earlier this year?

   → I _____*came to this city*_____ this year.

2. What is something you are doing this year?

   → I _____*am studying English*_____ this year.

3. What is something you are going to do this year?

   → I _____*am going to visit my relatives in Cairo*_____ this year.

4. What is something you did earlier today?

   → I _____ today.

5. What is something you are doing today, right now?

   → I _____ today.

6. What is something you are going to do later today?

   → I _____ today.

7. What is something you did earlier this morning / afternoon / evening?

   → I _____ this _____.

8. What is something you are going to do later this morning / afternoon / evening?

   → I _____ this _____.

■ **EXERCISE 13:**   Complete the sentences. Discuss the different VERB TENSES that are possible.

1. _____ today.

2. _____ this morning.

3. _____ this afternoon.

4. _____ this evening.

5. _____ tonight.

6. _____ this week.

7. _____ this month.

8. _____ this year.

■ **EXERCISE 14—ORAL:** In groups of three, ask classmates questions about future activities.

STUDENT A: Begin your question with "***When are you going to . . . ?***"
STUDENT B: Answer Student A's question.
STUDENT A: Ask Student C a question that begins with "***When is (. . .) going to . . . ?***"
STUDENT C: Answer in a complete sentence.

Example: go downtown
STUDENT A: When are you going to go downtown?
STUDENT B: This weekend. (Tomorrow morning. / In a couple of days. / Etc.)
STUDENT A: When is (. . .) going to go downtown?
STUDENT C: He/She is going to go downtown this weekend.

1. study at the library
2. go shopping
3. go to *(name of a class)*
4. have dinner
5. do your grammar homework
6. get married
7. go on a picnic
8. visit *(name of a place in this city)*

9. call (. . .) on the phone
10. go to *(name of restaurant)* for dinner
11. see your family again
12. quit smoking
13. buy a car
14. see (. . .)
15. go to *(name of a place in this city)*
16. take a vacation

■ **EXERCISE 15—ORAL:** In pairs, ask a classmate a question. Use the given words in your question.

Example: tomorrow morning
STUDENT A: Are you going to come to class tomorrow morning?
STUDENT B: Yes, I am. OR: No, I'm not.
Example: yesterday morning
STUDENT A: Did you eat breakfast yesterday morning?
STUDENT B: Yes, I did. OR: No, I didn't.

Switch roles.

1. last night
2. tomorrow night
3. tonight
4. tomorrow afternoon
5. yesterday afternoon
6. this afternoon
7. last Friday
8. next Friday
9. next week

10. last week
11. this week
12. yesterday morning
13. tomorrow morning
14. this morning
15. later today
16. a couple of hours ago
17. in a couple of hours *(from now)*
18. this evening

6-5 FUTURE TIME: USING *WILL*

STATEMENT	(a) Mike **will go** to the library tomorrow. (b) Mike **is going to go** to the library tomorrow.	(a) and (b) have basically the same meaning.
	(c) INCORRECT: *Mike will* **goes** *there.*	The simple form of a verb follows **will**. In (c): *goes* is NOT correct.
	(d) INCORRECT: *Mike will***s** *go there.*	There is never a final **-s** on **will** for future time.
	(e) INCORRECT: *Mike will* **to** *go there.*	**Will** is not followed by an infinitive with **to**.
CONTRACTIONS	(f) I will come. = **I'll** come. You will come. = **You'll** come. She will come. = **She'll** come. He will come. = **He'll** come. It will come. = **It'll** come. We will come = **We'll** come. They will come. = **They'll** come.	**Will** is contracted to **'ll** with subject pronouns.★ These contractions are common in both speaking and writing.
NEGATIVE	(g) Bob **will not be** here tomorrow. (h) Bob **won't be** here tomorrow.	Negative contraction: **will** + **not** = **won't**

★**Will** is also often contracted with nouns in speaking (but not in writing).
WRITTEN: *Tom will be here at ten.*
SPOKEN: *"Tom'll" be here at ten.*

■ **EXERCISE 16—ORAL:** Change the sentences by using **will** to express future time.

1. I'm going to arrive around six tomorrow.
   → *I'll arrive around six tomorrow.*
2. Fred isn't going to come to our party.
3. He's going to be out of town next week.
4. Sue is going to be in class tomorrow.
5. She has a cold, but she isn't going to stay home.
6. Jack and Peggy are going to meet us at the movie theater.
7. They're going to be there at 7:15.
8. Tina is going to stay home and watch TV tonight.★
9. This is an important letter. I'm going to send this letter by express mail.

★When two verbs are connected by *and*, the helping verbs **be going to** and **will** are usually not repeated. For example:
   I'm going to lock the doors and ~~am going to~~ turn out the lights.
   I'll lock the doors and ~~will~~ turn out the lights.

10. My parents are going to stay at a hotel in Honolulu.
11. Hurry up, or we're going to be late for the concert.
12. I'm not going to be at home this evening.
13. I'm going to wash the dishes and clean the kitchen after dinner.
14. Be careful with those scissors! You're going to hurt yourself!

6-6 ASKING QUESTIONS WITH *WILL*

QUESTION						ANSWER
(QUESTION + WORD)	*WILL* +	SUBJECT +	MAIN VERB			
(a)	*Will*	*Tom*	*come*	tomorrow?	→	*Yes, he will.*★ *No, he won't.*
(b)	*Will*	*you*	*be*	at home tonight?	→	*Yes, I will.*★ *No, I won't.*
(c) When	*will*	*Ann*	*arrive?*		→	*Next Saturday.*
(d) What time	*will*	*the plane*	*arrive?*		→	*Three-thirty.*
(e) Where	*will*	*you*	*be*	tonight?	→	*At home.*

*NOTE: *will* is not contracted with a pronoun in a short answer. See Chart 1-9 for information about the use of contractions in short answers.

■ **EXERCISE 17:** Make questions.

1. A: _____*Will you be at home tomorrow night?*_____

   B: Yes, _____*I will.*_____ (I'll be at home tomorrow night.)

2. A: _____*Will Ann be in class tomorrow?*_____

   B: No, _____*she won't.*_____ (Ann won't be in class tomorrow.)

3. A: _____ *When will you see Mr. Pong?* _____

   B: Tomorrow afternoon. (I'll see Mr. Pong tomorrow afternoon.)

4. A: _____

   B: Yes, _____ (The plane will be on time.)

5. A: _____

   B: Yes, _____ (Dinner will be ready in a few minutes.)

6. A: _____

   B: In a few minutes. (Dinner will be ready in a few minutes.)

7. A: _____

   B: Next year. (I'll graduate next year.)

8. A: _____

   B: At the community college. (Mary will go to school at the community college next year.)

9. A: _____

   B: No, _____ (Jane and Mark won't be at the party.)

10. A: _____

    B: Yes, _____ (Mike will arrive in Chicago next week.)

11. A: _____

    B: In Chicago. (Mike will be in Chicago next week.)

12. A: _____

    B: No, _____ (I won't be home early tonight.)

13. A: _____

    B: In a few minutes. (Dr. Smith will be back in a few minutes.)

14. A: _____

    B: Yes, _____ (I'll be ready to leave at 8:15.)

    A: Are you sure?

6-7 VERB SUMMARY: PRESENT, PAST, AND FUTURE

	STATEMENT	NEGATIVE	QUESTION
SIMPLE PRESENT	I *eat* lunch every day. He *eats* lunch every day.	I *don't eat* breakfast. She *doesn't eat* breakfast.	*Do* you *eat* breakfast? *Does* she *eat* lunch?
PRESENT PROGRESSIVE	I *am eating* an apple right now. She *is eating* an apple. They *are eating* apples.	I'*m not eating* a pear. She *isn't eating* a pear. They *aren't eating* pears.	*Am* I *eating* a banana? *Is* he *eating* a banana? *Are* they *eating* bananas?
SIMPLE PAST	He *ate* lunch yesterday.	He *didn't eat* breakfast.	*Did* you *eat* breakfast?
BE GOING TO	I *am going to eat* lunch at noon. She *is going to eat* lunch at noon. They *are going to eat* lunch at noon.	I'*m not going to eat* breakfast tomorrow. She *isn't going to eat* breakfast tomorrow. They *aren't going to eat* breakfast tomorrow.	*Am* I *going to see* you tomorrow? *Is* she *going to eat* lunch tomorrow? *Are* they *going to eat* lunch tomorrow?
WILL	He *will eat* lunch tomorrow.	He *won't eat* breakfast tomorrow.	*Will* he *eat* lunch tomorrow?

■ **EXERCISE 18—VERB REVIEW:** Complete the sentences with the verbs in parentheses.

1. Right now, Anita *(sit)* _____*is sitting*_____ at her desk.

2. She *(do, not)* _____ homework. She *(write)*

   _____ a letter to her parents.

3. She (write) _____ to her parents every week.

4. She (write, not) _____ a letter every day.

5. Her parents (expect, not) _____ to get a letter every day.

6. Last night Anita (write) _____ a letter to her brother. Then she

   (start) _____ to write a letter to her sister.

7. While Anita was writing a letter to her sister last night, her phone (ring)

   _____ . It (be) _____ her sister!

8. Anita (finish, not) _____ the letter to her sister last night.

   After she (talk) _____ to her sister, she (go) _____

   to bed.

9. Tomorrow she (write) _____ a letter to her cousin in Brazil.

10. Anita (write, not) _____ a letter to her parents tomorrow.

11. (you, write) _____ a letter to someone every day?

12. (you, write) _____ a letter to someone yesterday?

13. (you, write) _____ a letter to someone tomorrow?

6-8 VERB SUMMARY: FORMS OF *BE*

	STATEMENT	NEGATIVE	QUESTION
SIMPLE PRESENT	I *am* from Korea. He *is* from Egypt. They *are* from Venezuela.	I *am not* from Jordan. She *isn't* from China. They *aren't* from Italy.	*Am* I in the right room? *Is* she from Greece? *Are* they from Kenya?
SIMPLE PAST	Ann *was* late yesterday. They *were* late yesterday.	She *wasn't* on time. They *weren't* on time.	*Was* she in class? *Were* they in class?
BE GOING TO	I *am going to be* late. She *is going to be* late. They *are going to be* late.	I'*m not going to be* on time. She *isn't going to be* on time. They *aren't going to be* on time.	*Am* I *going to be* late? *Is* she *going to be* late? *Are* they *going to be* late tomorrow?
WILL	He *will be* at home tomorrow.	He *won't be* at work tomorrow.	*Will* he *be* at work next week?

■ **EXERCISE 19—REVIEW OF *BE*:**   Complete the sentences with the VERBS in parentheses.

1. I *(be)* _____ in class right now. I *(be, not)* _____

   _____ here yesterday. I *(be)* _____ absent

   yesterday. *(you, be)* _____ in class yesterday? *(Carmen, be)*

   _____ here yesterday?

2. Carmen and I *(be)* _____ absent from class yesterday. We

   (be, not) _____ here.

3. My friends *(be)* _____ at Fatima's apartment tomorrow

   evening. I *(be)* _____ there too. *(you, be)* _____

   there? *(Yuko, be)* _____ there?

4. A whale *(be, not)* _____ a fish. It *(be)* _____ a

   mammal. Dolphins *(be, not)* _____ fish either. They

   (be) _____ mammals.

DOLPHIN

■ **EXERCISE 20—VERB REVIEW:**   Complete the sentences with the verbs in parentheses. Give
short answers to questions where necessary.

1. A: *(you, have)* ____*Do you have*____ a bicycle?

   B: Yes, I *(do)* ____*do*____. I *(ride)* ____*ride*____ it to work
       every day.

2. A: *(you, walk)* _____ to work yesterday?

   B: No, I _____. I *(ride)* _____ my bicycle.

3. A: *(you, know)* _____ Mr. Park?

   B: Yes, I _____.

   A: Where *(you, meet)* _____ him?

   B: I *(meet)* _____ him at a dinner party at my uncle's house.

4. A: What time *(you, get up)* _____ every day?
   B: Between six and seven.

   A: What time *(you, get up)* _____ tomorrow?
   B: Six-thirty.

5. A: Where *(you, study, usually)* _____?
   B: In my room.

   A: *(you, go)* _____ to the library to study sometimes?

   B: No. I *(like, not)* _____ to study at the library.

6. A: *(you, be)* _____ in class tomorrow?

   B: Yes, I _____. But I *(be, not)* _____ in class
   the day after tomorrow.

7. A: *(Yuko, call)* _____ you last night?

   B: Yes, she _____. We *(talk)* _____ for a few minutes.

   A: *(she, tell)* _____ you about her brother?

   B: No, she _____. She *(say, not)* _____
   anything about her brother. Why?

   A: Her brother *(be)* _____ in an accident.
   B: That's too bad. What happened?

A: A dog *(run)* _____ in front of his bicycle. Her brother *(want, not)*

_____ to hit the dog. When he *(try)* _____

to avoid the dog, his bike *(run)* _____ into a truck. It was an
unfortunate accident.

B: *(he, be)* _____ in the hospital now?

A: No, he _____. He *(be)* _____ at home.

8. A: *(whales, breathe)* _____ air?

B: Yes, they _____.

A: *(a whale, have)* _____ lungs?

B: Yes, it _____.

A: *(a whale, be)* _____ a fish?

B: No, it _____. It *(be)* _____ a mammal.

9. A: *(you, watch)* _____ *Star Trek* on TV last night?
B: What's *Star Trek*?

A: It *(be)* _____ a TV show about

the future. It *(be)* _____ a
science fiction show. *(you, like)*

_____
science fiction?

B: Yes, I _____. I *(read)* _____ science fiction books

often. When *(Star Trek, be)* _____
on TV again?
A: Next week, on Thursday at nine o'clock.

B: I *(try)* _____ to watch it. I might like it. What *("trek," mean)*

_____?

A: "Trek" *(mean)* _____ a long and difficult journey.

B: What *("journey," mean)* _____?

A: "Journey" *(mean)* _____ that you travel from one place to another
place. *Star Trek* is the story of people who travel in outer space among the stars.

■ **EXERCISE 21—REVIEW (ORAL/WRITTEN):**   The name of the person in the pictures is Alex.
What is he doing? Why? Make up probable reasons. Give three different
descriptions of his activities according to the given directions.

1. DESCRIPTION #1: Assume the pictures show things that Alex is doing right now
    and/or does every day. Use the pictures to describe some of Alex's activities, using
    present tenses.

2. DESCRIPTION #2: Assume the pictures show things that Alex is going to do
    tomorrow. Describe these activities.

3. DESCRIPTION #3: Assume the pictures show things that Alex did yesterday. Describe
    these activities.

PRESENT			**What** + *a form of* **do** is used to ask about activities.
(a) *What* **do** you **do** every day?	→	I *work* every day.	
(b) *What* **are** you **doing** right now?	→	I'm *studying English*.	
PAST			
(c) *What* **did** you **do** yesterday?	→	I *went to school* yesterday.	
FUTURE			
(d) *What* **are** you **going to do** tomorrow? → I'm *going to go downtown* tomorrow.			
(e) *What* **will** we **do** if it rains tomorrow? → We'll *stay home* if it rains tomorrow.			

■ **EXERCISE 22:** Complete the sentences with the words in parentheses.

1. A: What (*you, do*) _____ *do you do* _____ every Friday?

   B: I (*come*) _____ *come* _____ to class.

2. A: What (*you, do*) _____ last Friday?

   B: I (*come*) _____ to class.

3. A: What (*you, do*) _____ next Friday?

   B: I (*come*) _____ to class.

4. A: What (*you, do*) _____ yesterday evening?

   B: I (*watch*) _____ TV.

5. A: What (*you, do*) _____ every evening?

   B: I (*watch*) _____ TV.

6. A: What (*you, do*) _____ tomorrow evening?

   B: I (*watch*) _____ TV.

7. A: What (*you, do*) _____ right now?

   B: I (*do*) _____ a grammar exercise.

8. A: What (*Maria, do*) _____ every morning?

   B: She (*go*) _____ to work.

9. A: What *(the students, do)* _____ right now?

   B: They *(work)* _____ on this exericse.

10. A: What *(they, do)* _____ in class tomorrow?

    B: They *(take)* _____ a test.

11. A: What *(Boris, do)* _____ last night?

    B: He *(go)* _____ to a movie.

12. A: What *(the teacher, do)* _____ every day at the beginning
    of class?

    B: She *(put)* _____ her books on her desk, *(look)* _____

    at the class, and *(say)* _____, "Good morning."

■ **EXERCISE 23—ORAL:** Ask a classmate a question. Use **What** + a form of **do** with the
given time expression.

   Example: yesterday
   STUDENT A: What did you do yesterday?
   STUDENT B: *(free response)*

   1. last night
   2. every day
   3. right now
   4. tomorrow
   5. yesterday afternoon
   6. tomorrow morning
   7. every morning

Switch roles.
   8. right now
   9. last Saturday
   10. next Saturday
   11. this morning
   12. this afternoon
   13. tonight
   14. next week

6-10 MAY/MIGHT VS. WILL

(a) It **may rain** tomorrow. (b) Anita **may be** at home *now*.	**May** + *verb* (simple form) expresses a possibility in the future, as in (a), or a present possibility, as in (b).
(c) It **might rain** tomorrow. (d) Anita **might be** at home *now*.	**Might** has the same meaning as **may**. (a) and (c) have the same meaning.
(e) Tom **will be** at the meeting tomorrow. (f) Ms. Lee **may/might be** at the meeting tomorrow.	In (e): The speaker uses **will** because he feels sure about Tom's presence at the meeting tomorrow. In (f): The speaker uses **may/might** to say, "I don't know if Ms. Lee will be at the meeting, but it is possible."
(g) Ms. Lee **may/might not be** at the meeting tomorrow.	Negative form: **may/might** + **not** NOTE: (f) and (g) have essentially the same meaning: Ms. Lee may or may not be at the meeting tomorrow.
(h) INCORRECT: *Ms. Lee **may will** be at the meeting tomorrow.* INCORRECT: *Ms. Lee **might will** be at the meeting tomorrow.*	**May** and **might** are not used with **will**.

■ **EXERCISE 24:** Complete the sentences. Use **will** or **won't** if you're sure. Use **may/might** if you're not sure.

1. I _____ be in class next Monday.
   - → *I **will be** in class next Monday.* = You're sure.
   - → *I **will not (won't) be** in class next Monday.* = You're sure.
   - → *I **may/might be** in class next Monday (or I **may/might not be** in class next Monday).* = It's possible, but you're not sure.

2. I _____ eat breakfast tomorrow morning.

3. I _____ be in class tomorrow.

4. I _____ get a letter from a friend of mine tomorrow.

5. I _____ watch TV for a little while after dinner tonight.

6. We _____ have a grammar test in class tomorrow.

7. I _____ eat dinner at a restaurant tonight.

8. It _____ be cloudy tomorrow.

9. The sun _____ rise tomorrow morning.

10. I _____ choose a career in music after I finish school.

11. There _____ be another earthquake in Japan in the next few months.

12. The population of the earth _____ continue to grow.

13. Cities _____ become more and more crowded.

14. We _____ communicate with beings from outer space before the end of the 21st century.

15. Do you think we _____ communicate with other beings through music?

■ **EXERCISE 25—WRITTEN:** Complete the sentences. Write about your activities *tomorrow*. Use **be going to** and **may/might**.

1. I'm going to get up at . . . tomorrow morning.
2. Then . . . .
3. After that . . . .
4. Around . . . o'clock . . . .
5. Later . . . .

6. At . . . o'clock . . . .
7. Then . . . .
8. After that . . . .
9. Next . . . .
10. Then at . . . o'clock . . . .

■ **EXERCISE 26—WRITTEN:** Complete the sentences. Write about your activities *yesterday*.

1. I got up at . . . yesterday morning.
2. I . . . and . . . .
3. Then I . . . .
4. I didn't . . . because . . . .
5. Later . . . .
6. Around . . . o'clock . . . .
7. Then . . . .

8. After that . . . .
9. At . . . o'clock . . . .
10. I didn't . . . because . . . .
11. At . . . I . . . .
12. . . . after that.
13. Then at . . . .

6-11 MAYBE (ONE WORD) VS. MAY BE (TWO WORDS)

(a) "Will Abdullah be in class tomorrow?" "I don't know. **Maybe. Maybe Abdullah will be** in class tomorrow, and **maybe he won't.**"	The adverb **maybe** (one word) means "possibly."

(b) | **Maybe**| | Abdullah | | will be | here.
  adverb   subject   verb
 	
 (c) | Abdullah | | **may be** | here tomorrow.
  subject   verb
	Maybe comes in front of a subject and verb.
	
	 May be (two words) is used as the verb of a sentence.

■ **EXERCISE 27:** Find the sentences where **maybe** is used as an adverb and where **may** is used as part of the verb.

1. Maybe it will rain tomorrow. → **maybe** = *an adverb*

2. It may rain tomorrow. → **may rain** = *a verb;* **may** *is part of the verb*

3. We may go to the art museum tomorrow.

4. Maybe Ann would like to go to the museum with us.

5. She may like to go to art museums.

6. It's cold and cloudy today. It may be cold and cloudy tomorrow. Maybe the weather will be warm and sunny this weekend.

■ **EXERCISE 28:** Use **maybe** or **may/might**.

1. A: Is David going to come to the party?

   B: I don't know. _____*Maybe*_____.

2. A: What are you going to do tomorrow?

   B: I don't know. I _____*may/might*_____ go swimming.

3. A: What are you going to do tomorrow?

   B: I don't have any plans. _____ I'll go swimming.

4. A: Where is Robert?

   B: I don't know. He _____ be at his office.

5. A: Where is Robert?

   B: I don't know. _____ he's at his office.

6. A: Are Kate and Steve going to get married?

   B: _____. Who knows?

7. A: Are you going to move to Portland or to Seattle?

   B: I don't know. I _____ move to San Francisco.

8. A: Where are you planning to go on your vacation?

   B: _____ we'll go to Mexico. We haven't decided yet. We

   _____ go to Florida.

9. A: Is Amanda married?

   B: Hmmm. I'm not sure. _____ she is, and

   _____ she isn't.

10. A: Do you think it will rain tomorrow?

    B: I have no idea. _____ it will, and _____ it won't.

11. A: Are you going to study English next semester?

    B: _____. Are you?

12. A: I'd like to have a pet.

    B: Oh? What kind of pet would you like to get?

    A: Oh, I don't know. I haven't decided yet. _____ I'll get a

    canary. Or _____ I'll get a snake. I'm not sure. I

    _____ get a frog. Or I _____ get a turtle.

    B: What's wrong with a cat or dog?

■ **EXERCISE 29:** Complete the sentences with **maybe** or **may be**.

1. A: I _____*may be*_____ a little late tonight.
   B: That's okay. I won't worry about you.

2. A: Will you be here by seven o'clock?

   B: It's hard to say. _____*Maybe*_____ I'll be a little late.

3. A: It _____ cold tomorrow.
   B: That's okay. Let's go to the beach anyway.

4. A: Will the plane be on time?

   B: I think so, but it _____ a few minutes late.

5. A: Do you want to go to the park tomorrow?
   B: Sure. That sounds like fun.

   A: Let's talk to Carlos too. _____ he would like to go with us.

6. A: Where's Mr. Chu?

   B: Look in Room 506 down the hall. I think he _____ there.

   A: No, he's not there. I just looked in Room 506.

   B: _____ he's in Room 508.

■ **EXERCISE 30—ORAL (BOOKS CLOSED):** Answer the question by using *I don't know* + *maybe* or *may/might*.

   Example: What are you going to do tonight?
   Response: I don't know. Maybe I'll watch TV. / I may watch TV. / I might watch TV.

   1. What are you going to do tonight?
   2. What are you going to do tomorrow?
   3. What are you going to do after class today?
   4. What are you going to do this weekend?
   5. What are you going to do this evening?
   6. Who is going to go shopping tomorrow? What are you going to buy?
   7. Who is going to go out to eat tonight? Where are you going to go?
   8. Who is going to get married? When?
   9. Who is going to watch TV tonight? What are you going to watch?
   10. Who is absent today? Where is he/she?
   11. Is it going to rain tomorrow? What is the weather going to be like tomorrow?
   12. Who is planning to go on a vacation? Where are you going to go?
   13. Who wants to have a pet? What kind of pet are you going to get?

■ **EXERCISE 31—ORAL (BOOKS CLOSED):** Use the given information to make guesses. Include *may/might* and *maybe* in some of your guesses.

   Example: (. . .) is absent today. Why? Do you have any possible explanations?
   → He/She **may be** sick. He/She **might be** out of town today. **Maybe** he/she is late today and will come soon.

   1. What is (. . .) going to do after class today?
   2. (. . .) said, "I have very exciting plans for this weekend." What is he/she going to do this weekend?
   3. (. . .) has an airplane ticket in his pocket. I saw it. Do you know where he/she is going to go?

4. (. . .) said, "I don't like it here in this city." Why doesn't (. . .) like it here? Do you have any idea?

5. (. . .) doesn't like it here. What is he/she going to do?

6. (. . .) has something very special in his/her pocket, but he/she won't show anyone what it is. What do you suppose is in his/her pocket?

7. Can you think of some good things that may happen to you this year?

8. What are some good things that might happen to (. . .) this year or next year?

9. Can you think of some bad things that might happen in this world this year or next?

10. What are some good things that may happen in the world this year?

11. What new inventions do you think we may have in the future to make our lives easier?

6-12 FUTURE TIME CLAUSES WITH *BEFORE, AFTER,* AND *WHEN*

(a) *Before Ann* **goes** *to work tomorrow,* she will eat breakfast.	In (a): *Before Ann goes to work tomorrow* is a future time clause.★
(b) INCORRECT: *Before Ann* **will go** *to work tomorrow, she will eat breakfast.* INCORRECT: *Before Ann* **is going to go** *to work tomorrow, she will eat breakfast.*	A future time clause uses the SIMPLE PRESENT TENSE, not **will** or **be going to.**
(c) I'm going to finish my homework *after I* **eat** *dinner tonight.*	In (c): *after I eat dinner tonight* = a future time clause.
(d) *When I* **go** *to New York next week,* I'm going to stay at the Hilton Hotel.	In (d): *When I go to New York next week* = a future time clause.

★See Chart 5-18 for information about time clauses.

■ **EXERCISE 32:** Find the time clauses.

1. When we go to the park tomorrow, we're going to go to the zoo.
   → *When we go to the park tomorrow = a time clause*

2. After I get home tonight, I'm going to make an overseas call to my parents.

3. Mr. Kim will finish his report before he leaves the office today.

4. I'll get some fresh fruit when I go to the market tomorrow.

5. Before I go to bed tonight, I'm going to write a letter to my brother.

6. I'm going to look for a job at a computer company after I graduate next year.

■ **EXERCISE 33:**   Complete the sentences with the words in parentheses.

1. Before I *(go)* _____*go*_____ to bed tonight, I *(watch)*

   _____*am going to watch/will watch*_____ my favorite show on TV.

2. I *(buy)* _____ a new coat when I *(go)* _____
   shopping tomorrow.

3. After I *(finish)* _____ my homework this evening, I *(take)*

   _____ a walk.

4. When I *(see)* _____ Eduardo tomorrow, I *(ask)* _____
   him to join us for dinner this weekend.

5. When I *(go)* _____ to Australia next month, I *(meet)*

   _____ my Aunt Emily for the first time.

6. Mrs. Polanski *(change)* _____ her clothes before she *(work)*

   _____ in her garden this afternoon.

■ **EXERCISE 34—ORAL (BOOKS CLOSED):** Give complete answers to the questions. Use time clauses.

Example: Who's going to go shopping later today? What are you going to do after you go shopping?
TEACHER: Who's going to go shopping later today?
STUDENT A: (*Student A raises his/her hand.*)
TEACHER: What are you going to do after you go shopping?
STUDENT A: After I go shopping, I'm going to go home. OR: I'm going to go home after I go shopping.
TEACHER: What is (. . .) going to do after he/she goes shopping?
STUDENT B: After (. . .) goes shopping, he/she is going to go home. OR: (. . .) is going to go home after he/she goes shopping.

1. Who's going to study tonight? What are you going to do after you study tonight?
2. Who else is going to study tonight? What are you going to do before you study?
3. Who's going to watch TV tonight? What are you going to do before you watch TV?
4. Who's going to watch TV tonight? What are you going to do after you watch TV?
5. Who's going to go shopping tomorrow? What are you going to buy when you go shopping tomorrow?
6. (. . .), what are you going to do tonight? What are you going to do before you . . . ? What are you going to do after you . . . tonight?
7. (. . .), what are you going to do tomorrow? What are you going to do before you . . . tomorrow? What are you going to do after you . . . tomorrow?
8. Who's going out of town soon? Where are you going? What are you going to do when you go to *(name of place)?*
9. Who's going to eat dinner tonight? What are you going to do before you eat dinner? What are you going to do after you eat dinner? What are you going to have when you eat dinner?
10. (. . .), what time are you going to get home today? What are you going to do before you get home? What are you going to do when you get home? What are you going to do after you get home?

6-13 CLAUSES WITH *IF*

(a)	**If it rains tomorrow,** `we will stay home.` *if*-clause main clause		An *if*-clause begins with *if* and has a subject and a verb.
(b)	`We will stay home` **if it rains tomorrow.** main clause *if*-clause		An *if*-clause can come before or after a main clause.
(c)	**If** it **rains** tomorrow, we won't go on a picnic.		The SIMPLE PRESENT (not **will** or **be going to**) is used in an *if*-clause to express future time.
(d)	I'm going to buy a new car next year **if I have** enough money. **If I don't have** enough money for a new car next year, I'm going to buy a used car.		

■ **EXERCISE 35:**   Complete the sentences with the words in parentheses.

1. If Ali *(be)* _____*is*_____ in class tomorrow, I *(ask)*

   _____*am going to/will ask*_____ him to join us for coffee after class.

2. If the weather *(be)* _____ nice tomorrow, I *(go)*

   _____ to Central Park with my friends.

3. I *(stay, not)* _____ home tomorrow if the weather *(be)*

   _____ nice.

4. If I *(feel, not)* _____ well tomorrow, I *(go, not)*

   _____ to work.

5. Masako *(stay)* _____ in bed tomorrow if she *(feel, not)*

   _____ well.

6. I *(stay)* _____ with my aunt and uncle if I *(go)*

   _____ to Miami next week.

7. If my friends *(be)* _____ busy tomorrow, I *(go)*

   _____ to a movie by myself.

8. If we *(continue)* _____ to pollute the land and oceans with poisons

   and waste, future generations *(suffer)* _____.

■ **EXERCISE 36—ORAL (BOOKS CLOSED):** In pairs, ask and answer questions.

STUDENT A: Your book is open. Ask a question that begins with "***What are you going to do . . . ?***"

STUDENT B: Your book is closed. Answer the question. Include the ***if***-clause in your answer.

Example: . . . if the weather is nice tomorrow?

STUDENT A: What are you going to do if the weather is nice tomorrow?

STUDENT B: If the weather is nice tomorrow, I'm going to sit outside in the sun. OR: I'm going to sit outside in the sun if the weather is nice tomorrow.

1. . . . if the weather is cold tomorrow?
2. . . . if the weather is hot tomorrow?
3. . . . if you don't understand a question that I ask you?
4. . . . if class is canceled tomorrow?
5. . . . if you don't feel well tomorrow?
6. . . . if you go to *(name of a place in this city)* tomorrow?

Switch roles.

7. . . . if it rains tonight?
8. . . . if you're hungry after class today?
9. . . . if you go to *(name of a place in this city)* tomorrow?
10. . . . if you don't study tonight?
11. . . . if you lose your grammar book?
12. . . . if someone steals your *(name of a thing: bicycle, wallet, etc.)*?

■ **EXERCISE 37:** Pair up with a classmate.

STUDENT A: Fill out the calendar with your activities for next week. (If you don't have many planned activities, invent some interesting ones.) Then give the calendar to Student B.

STUDENT B: In writing, describe Student A's activities next week. Try to include some time clauses beginning with ***when, after,*** and ***before***. Ask Student A questions about the activities on his/her calendar to get more information or clarification.

Example: *(Student A is Ali.)*

> **SUNDAY**
>
> 7:00 *tennis with Talal*
> 9:00 *breakfast with Talal*
> 1:00 *meet Ivan at Cozy's before game*
> 2:00 *Memorial Stadium*
>
> 7-9 *Study*

Student B interviews Student A about his calendar and then writes: On Sunday, Ali is going to play tennis with Talal early in the morning. They're going to play on the tennis courts here at this school. After they play tennis, they're going to have breakfast. In the afternoon, Ali is going to meet Ivan at Cozy's. Cozy's is a cafe. They're going to have a sandwich and a cup of coffee before they go to the soccer game at Memorial Stadium. Ali will study in the evening before he watches TV and goes to bed.

Fill out this calendar with your activities for next week.

MONDAY	THURSDAY
TUESDAY	**FRIDAY**
WEDNESDAY	**SATURDAY**

6-14 EXPRESSING HABITUAL PRESENT WITH TIME CLAUSES AND *IF*-CLAUSES

(a) FUTURE	After Ann **gets** to work today, she **is going to have** a cup of coffee.	(a) expresses a specific activity in the future. The SIMPLE PRESENT is used in the time clause. *Be going to* is used in the main clause.
(b) HABITUAL PRESENT	After Ann **gets** to work (every day), she always **has** a cup of coffee.	(b) expresses habitual activities, so the SIMPLE PRESENT is used in both the time clause and the main clause.
(c) FUTURE	If it **rains** tomorrow, I **am going to** wear my raincoat to school.	(c) expresses a specific activity in the future. The SIMPLE PRESENT is used in the *if*-clause. *Be going to* is used in the main clause.
(d) HABITUAL PRESENT	If it **rains**, I **wear** my raincoat.	(d) expresses habitual activities, so the SIMPLE PRESENT is used in both the *if*-clause and the main clause.

■ **EXERCISE 38:** Complete the sentences with the words in parentheses.

1. When I *(go)* _____ to Miami, I *(stay, usually)* _____ with my aunt and uncle.

2. When I *(go)* _____ to Miami next week, I *(stay)* _____ with my aunt and uncle.

3. Before I *(go)* _____ to class today, I *(have)* _____ a cup of tea.

4. Before I *(go)* _____ to class, I *(have, usually)* _____ a cup of tea.

5. I'm often tired in the evening after a long day at work. If I *(be)* _____ tired in the evening, I *(stay, usually)* _____ home and *(go)* _____ to bed early.

6. If I *(be)* _____ tired this evening, I *(stay)* _____ home and *(go)* _____ to bed early.

7. After I *(get)* _____ home in the evening, I *(sit, usually)* _____ in my favorite chair and *(read)* _____ the newspaper.

8. After I *(get)* _____ home tonight, I *(sit)* _____ in my favorite chair and *(read)* _____ the newspaper.

9. We *(go)* _____ swimming tomorrow if the weather *(be)* _____ warm.

10. My friends and I *(like)* _____ to go swimming if the weather *(be)* _____ warm.

11. People *(yawn, often)* _____ and *(stretch)* _____ when they *(wake)* _____ up.

12. I *(buy)* _____ some stamps when I *(go)* _____ to the post office this afternoon.

13. Before the teacher *(walk)* _____ into the room every day, there *(be)* _____ a lot of noise in the classroom.

14. When I *(go)* _____ to Taiwan next month, I *(stay)* _____

    with my friend Mr. Chu. After I *(leave)* _____ Taiwan, I *(go)*

    _____ to Hong Kong.

15. Ms. Wah *(go)* _____ to Hong Kong often. When she *(be)*

    _____ there, she *(like)* _____ to take the ferry across

    the bay, but sometimes she *(take)* _____ the subway under the bay.

■ **EXERCISE 39—ORAL (BOOKS CLOSED):** Answer the questions in complete sentences.

1. What do you do when you get up in the morning?
2. What are you going to do when you get up tomorrow morning?
3. What do you usually do before you go to bed?
4. What are you going to do before you go to bed tonight?
5. What are you going to do after you eat dinner tonight?
6. What do you usually do after you eat dinner?
7. What do you like to do if the weather is nice?
8. What are you going to do if the weather is nice tomorrow?

■ **EXERCISE 40:** Complete the sentences with your own words.

1. Before I go to bed tonight, ...
2. Before I go to bed, I usually . . . .
3. I'm going to . . . tomorrow after I . . . .
4. When I go to . . . , I'm going to . . . .
5. When I go to . . . , I always . . . .
6. If the weather . . . tomorrow, I . . . .
7. I will visit . . . when I . . . .
8. I'll . . . if I . . . .
9. If the weather . . . tomorrow, . . . you going to . . . ?
10. Are you going to . . . before you . . . ?
11. Do you . . . before you . . . ?
12. After I . . . tonight, I . . . .

■ **EXERCISE 41—REVIEW (ORAL/WRITTEN):** Pretend that you are going to start a self-improvement plan for this coming year. What are some things you are going to do/will do to improve yourself and your life this year? For example: *I will stop smoking. I am going to get more exercise. Etc.*

■ **EXERCISE 42—REVIEW (ORAL/WRITTEN):** What is going to happen in the lives of your classmates in the next 50 years? Make predictions about your classmates' futures. For example: *Heidi is going to become a famous research scientist. Ali will have a happy marriage and lots of children. Carlos will live in a quiet place and write poetry. Etc.*

■ **EXERCISE 43—REVIEW (ORAL/WRITTEN):** In the mail, you find a letter from a bank. In the envelope is a gift of a lot of money. (As a class, decide on the amount of money in the gift.) You can keep the money if you follow the directions in the letter. There are six different versions of the letter. Choose one (or more) of the letters and describe what you are going to do.

LETTER #1: You have to spend the money on a wonderful vacation. What are you going to do?

LETTER #2: You have to spend the money to help other people. What are you going to do?

LETTER #3: You have to spend the money to improve your school or place of work. What are you going to do?

LETTER #4: You have to spend the money on your family. What are you going to do?

LETTER #5: You have to spend the money to make the world a better place. What are you going to do?

LETTER #6: You have to spend the money to improve your country. What are you going to do?

6-15 MORE IRREGULAR VERBS

begin – began	*say – said*	*tell – told*
find – found	*sell – sold*	*tear – tore*
lose – lost	*steal – stole*	*wear – wore*
hang – hung		

■ **EXERCISE 44—ORAL (BOOKS CLOSED):** Practice using the IRREGULAR VERBS in the above list.

1. *begin–began* Our class begins at (9:00) every day. Class began at (9:00 this morning). When did class begin (this morning)?
   → *It began at (9:00).*
2. *lose–lost* Sometimes I lose things. Yesterday I lost my keys. What did I do yesterday?
3. *find–found* Sometimes I lose things. And then I find them. Yesterday I lost my keys, but then I found them in my jacket pocket. What did I do yesterday?

4. *tear–tore*   If we make a mistake when we write a check, we tear the check up. Yesterday I made a mistake when I wrote a check, so I tore it up and wrote a new check. What did I do yesterday?

5. *sell–sold*   People sell things that they don't need anymore. (. . .) has a new bicycle, so he/she sold his/her old bicycle. What did (. . .) do?

6. *hang–hung*   I like to hang pictures on my walls. This morning I hung a new picture in my bedroom. What did I do this morning?

7. *tell–told*   The kindergarten teacher likes to tell stories to her students. Yesterday she told a story about a little red train. What did the teacher do yesterday?

8. *wear–wore*   I wear a sweater to class every evening. Last night I wore a jacket as well. What did I wear last night?

9. *steal–stole*   Thieves steal money and other valuables. Last month a thief stole my aunt's pearl necklace. What did a thief do last month?

10. *say–said*   People usually say "hello" when they answer a phone. When (. . .) answered his/her phone this morning, he/she said "hello." What did (. . .) do this morning?

■ **EXERCISE 45:**   Complete the sentences. Use the words in parentheses.

begin	*say*	*tear*
find	*sell*	*tell*
hang	*steal*	*wear*
lose		

1. A: Did you go to the park yesterday?

   B: No. We stayed home because it _____ to rain.

2. A: Susie is in trouble.
   B: Why?

   A: She _____ a lie. Her mom and dad are upset.

3. A: Where did you get that pretty shell?

   B: I _____ it on the beach.

SHELLS

4. A: May I please have your homework?

   B: I don't have it. I _____ it.
   A: You what!?
   B: I can't find it anywhere.

5. A: Where's my coat?

   B: I _____ it up in the closet for you.

6. A: What happened to your sleeve?

   B: I _____ it on a nail.
   A: That's too bad.

7. A: Do you still have your bicycle?

   B: No. I _____ it because I
      needed some extra money.

8. A: It's hot in here.
   B: Excuse me? What did you say?

   A: I _____ , "It's hot in here."

9. A: Why did you take the bus to work this morning? Why didn't you drive?

   B: Because somebody _____ my car last night.
   A: Did you call the police?
   B: Of course I did.

10. A: Did you wear your blue jeans to the job interview?

    B: Of course not! I _____ a suit.

■ **EXERCISE 46:** Complete the sentences. Use the words in parentheses. Use any appropriate
   verb form.

1. A: *(you, be)* _____ at home tomorrow morning around ten?

   B: No. I *(be)* _____ out.

2. A: I *(lose)* _____ my sunglasses yesterday.
   B: Where?

   A: I *(think)* _____ that I *(leave)* _____ them on a table
      at the restaurant.

3. A: How are you getting along?

   B: Fine. I'm making a lot of friends, and my English *(improve)* _____.

4. A: Sometimes children tell little lies. You talked to Annie. *(she, tell)* _____

   _____ the truth, or *(she, tell)* _____ a lie?

   B: She *(tell)* _____ the truth. She's honest.

5. A: *(you, write)* _____ a letter to George yesterday?

   B: Yes, I did. I *(send)* _____ him a letter yesterday.

6. A: May I see the classified section of the newspaper?
   B: Sure. Here it is.

   A: Thanks. I (want) _____ (look) _____ at the want ads. I

   (need) _____ (find) _____ a new apartment.

```
┌──────────────────────────────────────┐
│  APTS., UNFURN.                        │
│  ───────────────────────────          │
│  2 BR. $725/mo. Lake St.               │
│  Near bus. All utils. incl.            │
│  No pets. 361-3663. eves.              │
└──────────────────────────────────────┘
```

7. A: Where (you, go) _____ yesterday?

   B: I (go) _____ to my cousin's house. I (see) _____

   Jean there and (talk) _____ to her for a while. And I (meet)

   _____ my cousin's neighbors, Mr. and Mrs. Bell. They're nice
   people. I like them.

8. A: What are you going to do tonight? (you, study) _____?

   B: No. I don't think so. I'm tired. I think I (watch) _____

   TV for a while, or maybe I (listen) _____ to some

   music. Or I might read a novel. But I (want, not, study) _____

   _____ tonight.

9. A: (you, do) _____ your homework last night?

   B: No. I (be) _____ too tired. I (go) _____ to bed early

   and (sleep) _____ for nine hours.

10. A: Good morning.
    B: Excuse me?

    A: I (say) _____, "Good morning."

    B: Oh! Good morning! I'm sorry. I (understand, not) _____
    you at first.

11. A: What did you do yesterday?

B: Well, I *(wake up)* _____ around nine and *(go)*

_____ shopping. While I was downtown, someone *(steal)*

_____ my purse. I *(take)* _____ a taxi home. When

I *(get)* _____ out of the taxi, I *(tear)* _____ my

blouse. I *(borrow)* _____ some money from my roommate to
pay the taxi driver.

A: Did anything good happen to you yesterday?

B: Hmmm. Let me think. Oh yes. I *(lose)* _____ my grammar book,

but I *(find)* _____ it later.

6-16 MORE IRREGULAR VERBS

cost – cost	*hit – hit*	*spend – spent*
cut – cut	*hurt – hurt*	*understand – understood*
forget –forgot	*lend – lent*	
give – gave	*make – made*	

■ **EXERCISE 47—ORAL (BOOKS CLOSED):** Practice using the IRREGULAR VERBS in the above list.

1. *cost-cost* I bought a hat yesterday. I paid (twenty dollars) for it. It cost (twenty dollars). What did I buy yesterday? How much did it cost?
   → *You bought a hat. It cost (twenty dollars).*

2. *give-gave* People give gifts when someone has a birthday. Last week, (. . .) had a birthday. I gave him/her *(something)*. What did I do?

3. *make-made* I make good chocolate cake. Last week I made a cake for (. . .)'s birthday. What did I do last week?

4. *cut-cut* (. . .) cuts vegetables when he/she makes a salad. Two nights ago, while he/she was making a salad, he /she cut his/her finger with the knife. What happened two nights ago?

5. *hurt-hurt* When I have a headache, my head hurts. Yesterday I had a headache. My head hurt yesterday. How did my head feel yesterday? How does your head feel when you have a headache?

6. *lend-lent* I lend money to my friends if they need it. Yesterday I lent *(a certain amount of money)* to (. . .). What did I do?

7. *forget-forgot* Sometimes I forget my wallet. Last night, I forgot it at a restaurant. What did I do last night?

8. *spend-spent* I usually spend Saturdays with my parents. Last Saturday, I spent the day with my friends instead. What did I do last Saturday?

9. *shut-shut*   I shut the garage door every night at 10:00 P.M. I shut it early last night. What did I do last night?

10. *understand-*   I always understand (. . .) when he/she speaks. He/She just
    understood   said something and I understood it. What just happened?

11. *hit-hit*   (. . .) lives in an apartment. His/Her neighbors are very noisy. When they make too much noise, (. . .) hits the wall with his/her hand. Last night he/she couldn't get to sleep because of the noise, so he/she hit the wall with his/her hand. What did (. . .) do last night? What does he/she usually do when his/her neighbors make too much noise?

■ **EXERCISE 48:**   Complete the sentences. Use the words in parentheses.

1. A: How much *(a new car, cost)* _____?

   B: It *(cost)* _____ a lot! New cars are expensive.

2. A: Did you get a ticket for the rock concert?

   B: Yes, and it was really expensive! It *(cost)* _____ fifty dollars.

3. A: Where's your dictionary?

   B: I *(give)* _____ it to Robert.

4. A: I had a car accident yesterday morning.
   B: What happened?

   A: I *(hit)* _____ a telephone pole.

5. A: May I have your homework, please?

   B: I'm sorry, but I don't have it. I *(forget)* _____ it.

   A: You *(forget)* _____ it!?

6. A: Did you eat breakfast?

   B: Yeah. I *(make)* _____ some scrambled eggs and toast for myself.

7. Jack *(put)* _____ on his clothes every morning.

8. Jack *(put)* _____ on his clothes this morning after he got up.

9. A: Did you enjoy going into the city to see a show?

   B: Yes, but I *(spend)* _____ a lot of money. I can't afford to do that very often.

10. A: May I see your dictionary?

    B: I don't have it. I *(lend)* _____ it to George.

11. A: Is that knife sharp?

   B: It's very sharp. It *(cut)* _____ anything easily.

12. A: I went to a barber this morning. He *(cut)* _____ my hair too short.
   B: It looks fine.

■ **EXERCISE 49—ORAL (BOOKS CLOSED):** Give the past form. Spell the past form. Make sentences using the past form.

   Example: come
   Response: came . . . C–A–M–E . . . I came to class this morning.

1. come	19. meet	37. forget
2. eat	20. speak	38. drive
3. stand	21. take	39. ride
4. understand	22. wear	40. run
5. drink	23. write	41. go
6. break	24. fly	42. see
7. hear	25. leave	43. sit
8. lose	26. pay	44. cut
9. find	27. cost	45. hit
10. begin	28. spend	46. sing
11. put	29. sell	47. bring
12. shut	30. buy	48. read
13. hang	31. ring	49. teach
14. tell	32. make	50. think
15. tear	33. do	51. have
16. get	34. say	52. sleep
17. wake up	35. catch	53. give
18. steal	36. send	54. lend

■ **EXERCISE 50—REVIEW:** Complete the sentences. Use the words in parentheses. Use any appropriate verb form.

1. A: I *(cut)* _____ class tomorrow.
   B: Why?
   A: Why not?
   B: That's not a very good reason.

2. A: How did you get here?

   B: I *(take)* _____ a plane. I *(fly)* _____ here from Bangkok.

3. A: How do you usually get to class?

   B: I *(walk, usually)* _____, but sometimes I *(take)*

      _____ the bus.

4. A: Where *(you, meet)* _____ your wife?

   B: I *(meet)* _____ her at a party ten years ago.

5. A: Did you see that?
   B: What?

   A: The man in the red shirt *(hit)* _____ the man in the blue shirt.
   B: Really?

6. A: Were you late for the movie?

   B: No. The movie *(begin)* _____ at 7:30, and we *(get)* _____
      to the theater at 7:26.

7. A: What time *(the movie, begin)* _____ last
      night?
   B: 7:30.

   A: *(you, be)* _____ late?

   B: No. We *(make)* _____ it in time.

8. A: Do you hear that noise?
   B: What noise?

   A: *(you, listen)* _____?

9. A: Where's your homework?

   B: I *(lose)* _____ it.
   A: Oh?

   B: I *(forget)* _____ it.
   A: Oh?

   B: I *(give)* _____ it to Roberto to give to you, but he *(lose)*

      _____ it.
   A: Oh?

   B: Someone *(steal)* _____ it.
   A: Oh?

   B: Well, actually I *(have, not)* _____ enough time to
      finish it last night.
   A: I see.

10. A: Where's my book! Someone *(steal)* _____ it!

    B: Take it easy. Your book *(be)* _____ right here.
    A: Oh.

11. A: *(you, stay)* _____ here during vacation
    next week?

    B: No. I *(take)* _____ a trip to Miami. I *(visit)*

    _____ my aunt and uncle.

    A: How long *(you, be)* _____ away?
    B: About five days.

12. A: Why *(you, wear)* _____ a cast on your
    foot?

    B: I *(break)* _____ my ankle.
    A: How?

    B: I *(step)* _____ in a hole while I was running in the park.

13. A: *(you, want, go)* _____ to the zoo this
    afternoon?
    B: I'd like to go, but I can't because I have to study.
    A: That's too bad.

    B: *(you, go)* _____ to the zoo?

    A: Yes. The weather is perfect, and I *(want)* _____ *(get)*

    _____ outside and *(enjoy)* _____ it.

14. A: *(you, see)* _____ Randy yesterday?

    B: No, but I *(speak)* _____ to him on the phone. He *(call)*

    _____ me yesterday evening.
    A: Is he okay?
    B: Yes. He still has a cold, but he's feeling much better.
    A: That's good.

15. A: Is Carol here?

    B: No, she *(be, not)* _____. She *(leave)* _____ a few
    minutes ago.

    A: *(she, be)* _____ back soon?
    B: I think so.

    A: Where *(she, go)* _____?

    B: She *(go)* _____ to the drugstore.

■ **EXERCISE 51—REVIEW:** Choose the correct completions.

1. "Are you going to go to the baseball game tomorrow afternoon?"

   "I don't know. I _____."
      A. will   B. am going to   C. maybe   D. might

2. "Are Jane and Eric going to be at the meeting?"

   "No, they're too busy. They _____ be there."
      A. don't   B. won't   C. will   D. may

3. "Are you going to go to the market today?"

   "No. I went there _____ Friday."
      A. yesterday   B. next   C. last   D. ago

4. "When are you going to go to the bank?"

   "I'll go there before I _____ to the post office tomorrow morning."
      A. will go   B. go   C. went   D. am going

5. "Why is the teacher late today?"

   "I don't know. _____ he slept late."
      A. May   B. Did   C. Maybe   D. Was

6. "Do you like to go to New York City?"

   "Yes. When I'm in New York, I always _____ new things to do and places to
   go."
      A. found   B. find   C. will find   D. am finding

7. "Is Ken going to talk to us this afternoon about our plans for tomorrow?"

   "No. He'll _____ us this evening."
      A. calls   B. calling   C. call   D. called

8. "_____ are you going to do after class today?"
   "I'm going to go home."
      A. When   B. Where   C. What   D. What time

9. "Where _____ Ivonne live before she moved into her new apartment?"
   "She lived in a dormitory at the university."
      A. did   B. does   C. is   D. was

10. "What time _____ Olga and Boris going to arrive?"
    "Six."
      A. is   B. do   C. will   D. are

■ **EXERCISE 52—REVIEW (ERROR ANALYSIS):**   Correct the errors in the sentences.

1. Is Ivan will go to work tomorrow?

2. When you will call me?

3. Will Tom to meet us for dinner tomorrow?

4. We went to a movie yesterday night.

5. If it will be cold tomorrow morning, my car won't start.

6. We maybe late for the concert tonight.

7. Did you found your keys?

8. What time you are going to come tomorrow?

9. My sister is going to meet me at the airport. My brother won't to be there.

10. Fatima will call us tonight when she will arrive home safely.

11. Mr. Wong will sells his business and retires next year.

12. Do you will be in Venezuela next year?

13. Emily may will be at the party.

14. I'm going to return home in a couple of month.

15. When I'll see you tomorrow, I'll return your book to you.

16. I saw Jim three day ago.

17. I may to don't be in class tomorrow.

18. Ahmed puts his books on his desk when he walked into his apartment.

19. A thief stoled my bicycle.

20. I'll see my parents when I will return home for a visit next July.

■ **EXERCISE 53—REVIEW:** Complete the sentences. Use the words in parentheses. Use any appropriate verb form.

(1)   *Peter and Rachel are brother and sister. Right now their parents* (be) _____

(2)   *abroad on a trip, so they* (stay) _____ *with their grandmother. They*

(3)   (like) _____ *to stay with her. She* (make, always) _____

(4)   *wonderful food for them. And she* (tell) _____ *them stories every night before they*

(5)   (go) _____ *to bed.*

(6)   *Before Peter and Rachel* (go) _____ *to bed last night, they* (ask)

(7)   _____ *Grandma to tell them a story. She* (agree) _____. *The*

(8)   *children* (put) _____ *on their pajamas,* (brush) _____ *their teeth, and*

(9)   (sit) _____ *with their grandmother in her big chair to listen to a story.*

GRANDMA: That's good. Sit here beside me and get comfortable.

(10)   CHILDREN: What *(you, tell)* _____ us about tonight,

         Grandma?

(11)   GRANDMA: Before I *(begin)* _____ the story, I *(give)* _____

         each of you a kiss on the forehead because I love you very much.

(12)   CHILDREN: We *(love)* _____ you, too, Grandma.

(13)   GRANDMA: Tonight I *(tell)* _____ you a story about Rabbit and

Eagle. Ready?

    CHILDREN: Yes!

    GRANDMA: Rabbit had light gray fur and a white tail. He lived with his family in a hole

(14)   in a big, grassy field. Rabbit *(be)* _____ afraid of many things, but he

(15)   *(be)* _____ especially afraid of Eagle. Eagle liked to eat rabbits for dinner.

(16)   One day while Rabbit was eating grass in the field, he *(see)* _____ Eagle in

(17)   the sky above him. Rabbit *(be)* _____ very afraid and *(run)* _____

(18)   home to his hole as fast as he could. Rabbit *(stay)* _____ in his hole day

(19)   after day because he *(be)* _____ afraid to go outside. He *(get)* _____

(20)   very hungry, but still he *(stay)* _____ in his hole. Finally, he *(find)*

(21)   _____ the courage to go outside because he *(need)* _____

(22)   *(eat)* _____ .

(23)   Carefully and slowly, he *(put)* _____ his little pink nose outside the

(24)   hole. He *(smell, not)* _____ any dangerous animals.

(25)   And he *(see, not)* _____ Eagle anywhere, so he *(hop)*

(26)   _____ out and *(find)* _____ some delicious new

(27)   grass to eat. While he was eating the grass, he *(see)* _____ a shadow on the

(28)   field and *(look)* _____ up. It was Eagle! Rabbit said, "Please don't eat

me, Eagle! Please don't eat me, Eagle!"

On this sunny afternoon, Eagle was on her way home to her nest when she

(29) *(hear)* _____ a faint sound below her. "What is that sound?" Eagle said

(30) to herself. She looked around, but she *(see, not)* _____

(31) anything. She *(decide)* _____ to ignore the sound and go home.

(32) She was tired and *(want)* _____ *(rest)* _____ in

her nest.

(33) Then below her, Rabbit *(say)* _____ again in a very loud voice,

"Please don't eat me, Eagle! Please don't eat me, Eagle." This time Eagle *(hear)*

(34) _____ Rabbit clearly. Eagle *(spot)* _____ Rabbit in

(35) the field, *(fly)* _____ down, and *(pick)* _____ Rabbit

up in her talons.

"Thank you, Rabbit," said Eagle. "I was hungry and *(know, not)*

(36) _____ where I could find my dinner. It's a good thing

(37) you called to me." Then Eagle *(eat)* _____ Rabbit for dinner.

(38) There's a lesson to learn from this story, children. If you *(be)* _____

afraid and expect bad things to happen, bad things will happen. The opposite is also

(39) true. If you *(expect)* _____ good things to happen, good things will happen.

(40) *(you, understand)* _____? Now it's time for bed.

CHILDREN: Please tell us another story!

(41) GRANDMA: Not tonight. I'm tired. After I *(have)* _____ a warm drink, I

(42) *(go)* _____ to bed. All of us need *(get)* _____ a

(43) good night's sleep. Tomorrow *(be)* _____ a busy day.

(44) CHILDREN: What *(we, do)* _____ tomorrow?

(45) GRANDMA: After we *(have)* _____ breakfast, we *(go)* _____

(46) to the zoo at Woodland Park. When we *(be)* _____ at the zoo, we

(47) *(see)* _____ lots of wonderful animals. Then in the afternoon

(48) we *(see)* _____ a play at the Children's Theater. But before we

(49) *(see)* _____ the play, we *(have)* _____

a picnic lunch in the park.

(50) CHILDREN: Wow! We *(have)* _____ a wonderful day tomorrow!

GRANDMA: Now off to bed! Goodnight, Rachel and Peter. Sleep tight.★

CHILDREN: Goodnight, Grandma. Thank you for the story!

★"Sleep tight" means "sleep well; have a good night's sleep."

CHAPTER 7
Expressing Ability

7-1 USING *CAN*

(a) I have some money. I **can buy** a book. (b) We have time and money. We **can go** to a movie. (c) Tom is strong. He **can lift** the heavy box.	**Can** expresses *ability* and *possibility*.
(d) CORRECT: Yuko can **speak** English.	The simple form of the main verb follows **can**. In (d): *speak* is the main verb.
(e) INCORRECT: *Yuko can **to** speak English.*	An infinitive with **to** does NOT follow **can**. In (e): *to speak* is incorrect.
(f) INCORRECT: *Yuko can speak**s** English.*	The main verb never has a final **-s**. In (f): *speaks* is incorrect.

(g) Alice **can not** come.
Alice **cannot** come.
Alice **can't** come.
	NEGATIVE:
	    can + **not** = **can not** OR: **cannot**
	CONTRACTION:
	    can + **not** = **can't**

■ **EXERCISE 1—ORAL:** Make sentences from the given words. Use **can** or **can't**.

Example: A bird \ sing   *Example:* A horse \ sing
Response: A bird can sing.   *Response:* A horse can't sing.

1. A bird \ fly
2. A cow \ fly
3. A child \ drive a car
4. An adult \ drive a car
5. A newborn baby \ walk
6. A fish \ breathe air
7. A fish \ swim

8. A deaf person \ hear
9. A blind person \ see
10. An elephant \ swim
11. An elephant \ climb trees
12. A cat \ climb trees
13. A boat \ float on water
14. A rock \ float on water

■ **EXERCISE 2—ORAL:** Make sentences about yourself using *I can* or *I can't*.

Example: speak Chinese
Response: I can speak Chinese. OR: I can't speak Chinese.

1. whistle
2. ride a bicycle
3. touch my ear with my elbow
4. play the piano*
5. play the guitar
6. lift a piano
7. drive a stick-shift car
8. fix a flat tire
9. swim
10. float on water
11. ski
12. do arithmetic
13. make a paper airplane
14. sew a button on a shirt
15. eat with chopsticks
16. wiggle my ears

7-2 USING *CAN*: QUESTIONS

(QUESTION WORD) + *CAN* + SUBJECT + MAIN VERB						ANSWER
(a)		*Can*	*you*	*speak*	Arabic? →	*Yes, I can.*
					→	*No, I can't.*
(b)		*Can*	*Marge*	*come*	to the party? →	*Yes, she can.*
					→	*No, she can't.*
(c)	*Where*	*can*	*I*	*buy*	a hammer? →	*At a hardware store.*
(d)	*When*	*can*	*you*	*help*	me? →	*Tomorrow afternoon.*

■ **EXERCISE 3:** Make yes/no questions. Give short answers.

1. A: ___*Can Jean speak English?*___

   B: ___*Yes, she can.*___ (Jean can speak English.)

2. A: ___*Can you speak French?*___

   B: ___*No, I can't.*___ (I can't speak French.)

3. A: _____

   B: _____ (Jim can't play the piano.)

4. A: _____

   B: _____ (I can whistle.)

_____

*In expressions with **play**, **the** is usually used with musical instruments: *play the piano, play the guitar, play the violin, etc.*

5. A: _____

   B: _____ (I can go shopping with you this afternoon.)

6. A: _____

   B: _____ (Carmen can't ride a bicycle.)

7. A: _____

   B: _____ (Elephants can swim.)

8. A: _____

   B: _____ (The students can finish this exercise quickly.)

9. A: _____

   B: _____
      (I can stand on my head.)

10. A: _____

    B: _____
       (The doctor can see you tomorrow.)

11. A: _____

    B: _____
       (We can't have pets in the dormitory.)

■ **EXERCISE 4—ORAL:**   Pair up with a classmate.
   STUDENT A: Your book is open. Ask a question. Use *"**Can you . . . ?**"*
   STUDENT B: Your book is closed. Answer the question.

   Example: speak Arabic
   STUDENT A: Can you speak Arabic?
   STUDENT B: Yes, I can. OR: No, I can't.

                                    Switch roles.
   1. ride a bicycle   11. spell Mississippi
   2. ride a motorcycle   12. see the back of (. . .)'s head
   3. ride a horse   13. count to five in *(a language)*
   4. play the piano   14. stand on your head
   5. play the guitar   15. touch your knee with your nose
   6. touch the ceiling of this room   16. touch your ear with your elbow
   7. cook *(a nationality)* food 17. play the violin
   8. sing   18. drive a stick-shift car
   9. whistle   19. fix a flat tire
   10. float on water   20. ski

■ **EXERCISE 5—ORAL:** Pair up with a classmate.
   STUDENT A: Your book is open. Ask a question. Use "*Where can I . . . ?*"
   STUDENT B: Your book is closed. Answer the question.

Example: buy a notebook
STUDENT A: Where can I buy a notebook?
STUDENT B: At the bookstore. / At *(name of a local store)*. / Etc.

Switch roles.

1. buy a camera
2. get a dozen eggs
3. buy a window fan
4. get a good dinner
5. go swimming
6. play tennis
7. catch a bus
8. mail a package

9. buy a diamond ring
10. buy a hammer
11. see a zebra
12. get a newspaper
13. find an encyclopedia
14. get a taxi
15. get a sandwich
16. cash a check

7-3   USING *KNOW HOW TO*

(a) I can swim.	(a) and (b) have basically the same meaning. ***Know how to*** expresses ability.
(b) I ***know how to swim***.	
(c) Can you cook?	(c) and (d) have basically the same meaning.
(d) ***Do*** you ***know how to cook***?	

■ **EXERCISE 6—ORAL:** Pair up with a classmate.
   STUDENT A: Your book is open. Ask a question. Use ***know how to*** in your question.
   STUDENT B: Your book is closed. Answer the question.

Example: swim
STUDENT A: Do you know how to swim?
STUDENT B: Yes, I do. OR: No, I don't.

Switch roles.

1. cook
2. dance
3. play the piano
4. get to the post office from here
5. fix a flat tire
6. drive a stick-shift car
7. wiggle your ears
8. sew

9. play the guitar
10. get to the airport from here
11. get to *(name of a store)* from here
12. use a hammer
13. use a screwdriver
14. count to five in *(a language)*
15. add, subtract, multiply, and divide
16. find the square root of nine

■ **EXERCISE 7—ORAL/WRITTEN:** Walk around and talk to your classmates. Ask them questions. Find people who have the abilities listed below. Ask them questions about their abilities. Write a report of the information you get from your classmates.

1. play a musical instrument
2. play a sport
3. speak three or four languages
4. cook
5. sing
6. sew
7. fix a car
8. draw
9. swim
10. eat with chopsticks

7-4	USING *COULD:* PAST OF *CAN*

(a) I am in Hawaii. I can go to the beach every day. (b) I was in Hawaii **last month**. I **could go** to the beach every day when I was there.	*could* = the past form of *can*.
(c) I can't go to the movie today. I have to study. (d) I $\begin{Bmatrix} \textbf{\textit{couldn't go}} \\ \textbf{\textit{could not go}} \end{Bmatrix}$ to the movie **last night**. I had to study.	NEGATIVE: *could* + *not* = *couldn't*
(e) **Could** you **speak** English before you came here?	QUESTION: *could* + *subject* + *main verb*

■ **EXERCISE 8:** Complete the sentences by using *couldn't*. Use the expressions in the list or your own words.

call you	*go to the movie*
come to class	*light the candles*
✔ *do my homework*	*listen to music*
get into my car	*wash his clothes*
go swimming	*watch TV*

1. I _____*couldn't do my homework*_____ last night because I was too tired.

2. I _____ yesterday because I lost your telephone number.

3. I _____ last night because my TV set is broken.

4. Tom _____ because he didn't have any matches.

5. The teacher _____ yesterday because he was sick.

6. I _____ last night because my radio doesn't work.

7. Ken _____ because he didn't have any laundry soap.

8. We _____ yesterday because the water was too cold.

9. I _____ yesterday because I locked all the doors and left the keys inside.

10. I _____ last night because I had to study.

■ **EXERCISE 9—ORAL (BOOKS CLOSED):** Answer the questions. Use *"No, I couldn't . . . because . . . ."*

> *Example:* Did you finish your homework last night?
> *Response:* No, I couldn't finish my homework because (I had a headache, etc.).

1. go shopping yesterday
2. study last night
3. go swimming yesterday
4. watch TV last night
5. go to (. . .)'s party last night
6. come to class yesterday
7. go downtown yesterday afternoon
8. wash your clothes yesterday

■ **EXERCISE 10—ORAL (BOOKS CLOSED):** What are some negative results in the given situations? Use **can't** or **couldn't**.

> *Example:* There's no chalk in the classroom.
> *Response:* We can't write on the board.

> *Example:* There was no chalk in the classroom yesterday.
> *Response:* The teacher couldn't write on the board.

1. (. . .) has a broken leg.
2. (. . .) had the flu last week.
3. (. . .) has only *(a small amount of money)* in his pocket/in her purse today.
4. (. . .) doesn't know how to use a computer.
5. Your parents had rules for you when you were a child.
6. All of you are adults. You are not children.
7. You didn't know any English last year.
8. Millions of people in the world live in poverty.

■ **EXERCISE 11:** Correct the errors in the following sentences.

1. Could you to drive a car when you were thirteen years old?

2. If your brother goes to the graduation party, he can meets my sister.

3. Mr. Lo was born in Hong Kong, but now he lives in Canada. He cannot understand spoken English before he moved to Canada, but now he speak and understand English very well.

4. I couldn't opened the door because I didn't have a key.

5. When Ernesto arrived at the airport last Tuesday, he can't find the right gate.

6. Please turn up the radio. I can't to hear it.

7-5 USING *VERY* AND *TOO* + ADJECTIVE

(a) The box is *very* heavy, but Tom *can* lift it. (b) The box is *too* heavy. Bob *can't* lift it. (c) The coffee is *very* hot, but I *can* drink it. (d) The coffee is *too* hot. I *can't* drink it.	*Very* and *too* come in front of adjectives; *heavy* and *hot* are adjectives. *Very* and *too* do NOT have the same meaning. In (a): *very heavy* = It is difficult but possible for Tom to lift the box. In (b): *too heavy* = It is impossible for Bob to lift it.

(e) The coffee is *too* hot.
    NEGATIVE RESULT: I can't drink it.
(f) The weather is *too* cold.
    NEGATIVE RESULT: We can't go to the beach.
	In the speaker's mind, the use of *too* implies a negative result.

TOM

BOB

■ **EXERCISE 12:** Complete the sentences. Use the expressions in the list or your own words.

> | | |
> |---|---|
> | *buy it* | *lift it* |
> | *do his homework* | *reach the cookie jar* |
> | *eat it* | *sleep* |
> | *go swimming* | *take a break* |

1. The soup is too hot. I can't _____

2. The diamond ring is too expensive. I can't _____

3. The weather is too cold. We can't _____

4. Peggy is too short.

   She can't _____

5. Ali is too tired.

   He can't _____

6. I am too busy.

   I can't _____

7. It's too noisy in the dorm at night.

   I can't _____

8. A piano is too heavy.

   I can't _____

■ **EXERCISE 13:** Complete the sentences. Use *too*. Use ADJECTIVES in the list or your own
words.

> | | |
> |---|---|
> | *cold* | *small* |
> | *expensive* | *tall* |
> | *heavy* | *tired* |
> | *noisy* | *young* |

1. You can't lift a car. A car is _____

2. Jimmy is ten. He can't drive a car. He's _____

3. I can't study in the dorm at night. It's _____

4. I don't want to go to the zoo. The weather is _____

5. Ann doesn't want to play tennis this afternoon. She's _____

6. I can't buy a new car. A new car is _____

7. John has gained weight. He can't wear his old shirt. It's _____

8. The basketball player can't stand up straight in the subway. He's _____

■ **EXERCISE 14:**   Complete the sentences. Use *too* or *very*.

1. The tea is _____*very*_____ hot, but I can drink it.

2. The tea is _____*too*_____ hot. I can't drink it.

3. I can't put my dictionary in my pocket. My dictionary is _____ big.

4. An elephant is _____ big. A mouse is _____ small.

5. I can't buy a boat because it's _____ expensive.

6. A sports car is _____ expensive, but Anita can buy one if she wants to.

7. We went to the Rocky Mountains for our vacation. The mountains are

   _____ beautiful.

8. I can't eat this food because it's _____ salty.

9. Amanda doesn't like her room in the dorm. She thinks it's _____ small.

10. I lost your dictionary. I'm _____ sorry. I'll buy you a new one.

11. A: Do you like your math course?

    B: Yes. It's _____ difficult, but I enjoy it.

12. A: Do you like your math course?

    B: No. It's _____ difficult. I don't like it because I can't understand the math.

13. A: It's seven-thirty. Do you want to go to the movie?

    B: We can't. It's _____ late. The movie started at seven.

14. A: Did you enjoy your dinner last night?

    B: Yes. The food was _____ good!

15. A: Are you going to buy that dress?

    B: No. It doesn't fit. It's _____ big.

16. A: Do you think Carol is smart?

    B: Yes, I do. I think she's _____ intelligent.

17. A: My daughter wants to get married.

    B: What? But she can't! She's _____ young.

18. A: Can you read that sign across the street?

    B: No, I can't. It's _____ far away.

7-6 USING *TOO MANY* AND *TOO MUCH* + NOUN

My stomach doesn't feel good. (a) I ate **too many sandwiches**. (b) I ate **too much food**.	**Too** is frequently used with **many** and **much**. **Too many** is used in front of count nouns, as in (a). **Too much** is used in front of noncount nouns, as in (b).*

*See Chart 4-6 for more information about count nouns and noncount nouns.

■ **EXERCISE 15:** Complete the sentences. Use **too many** or **too much**. Use **too many** with plural COUNT NOUNS. Use **too much** with NONCOUNT NOUNS.

1. I can't go to the movie tonight. I have _____*too much*_____ homework to do.

2. Mr. and Mrs. Smith have six cars. They have _____*too many*_____ cars.

3. Alex is nervous and jumpy. He drinks _____ coffee.

4. There are _____ students in my chemistry class. I can't remember all of their names.

5. Fred is a commuter. He drives to and from work every day. Yesterday afternoon he tried to get home early, but he couldn't because there was _____ traffic. There were _____ cars on the highway during rush hour.

6. You use _____ salt on your food. A lot of salt isn't good for you.

7. It's not possible for a person to have _____ friends.

8. The restaurant was crowded, so we left. There were _____ people at the restaurant.

9. This food is too hot! I can't eat it. There's _____ pepper in it.

10. Mike is gaining weight because he eats _____ food.

11. I can't buy this watch. It costs _____ money.

12. Ann doesn't study because she's always busy. She has _____ boyfriends.

13. I have to study for eight hours every night. My teachers assign _____ homework.

14. I invited three friends to my house for lunch. I made twelve sandwiches for them, but they ate only six. I made _____ sandwiches. I made _____ food for my guests.

■ **EXERCISE 16—ORAL (BOOKS CLOSED):**   Think of possible answers to the questions.

Example: You had too much homework last night. What was the result?
Response: I couldn't finish it. / I didn't get to bed until after midnight. / Etc.

1. (. . .) wants to buy *(something)*, but it costs too much money. What's the result?

2. (. . .) tried to read an article in the newspaper about *(a current topic)*, but there was too much vocabulary that he didn't know. What was the result?

3. (. . .) and (. . .) wanted to eat at *(name of a local restaurant)* last night, but there were too many people there. What was the result?

4. (. . .) likes to study in peace and quiet. His/Her roommate likes to listen to loud music and makes too much noise. What's the result?

5. (. . .) wants to *(do something)* today, but the weather is too (hot / cold / humid / cloudy / wet / etc.). What's the result?

6. (. . .) invited (. . .) to *(do something)* last night, but (. . .) was too busy. He/She had too much homework. What was the result?

7. Sometimes (. . .) drinks too much coffee. What's the result?

8. (. . .) wants to climb *(name of a mountain)*, but the mountain is too steep and too high. The climb is too difficult for (. . .) because he/she is an inexperienced climber. What is the result?

9. (. . .) took the bus yesterday. He/She was very tired and needed to sit down, but there were too many people on the bus. What was the result?

10. (. . .) made a cup of coffee for (. . .), but it was too strong. It tasted bitter. What was the result?

11. At the present rates of population growth, someday there will be too many people on earth. What will be the result?

12. (. . .)'s apartment is too small for him/her and his/her wife/husband (and their children). What's the result?

13. (. . .) took a trip to *(name of a place)* last month. He/She took six big suitcases. In other words, he/she had too many suitcases. What was the result?

7-7   USING *TOO* + ADJECTIVE + INFINITIVE

(a) Susie can't go to school because she is too young. (b) Susie is **too young to go** to school.	(a) and (b) have the same meaning.
TOO + ADJECTIVE + INFINITIVE (c) Susie is **too** **young** **to go** to school. (d) Peggy is **too** **short** **to reach** the cookie jar. (e) Bob is **too** **tired** **to do** his homework.	

■ **EXERCISE 17:**   Make sentences with the same meaning by using an infinitive after **too** +
ADJECTIVE.

1. Mr. Cook is old. He can't drive a car anymore.

   → Mr. Cook is ⌊___*too*___⌋ ⌊___*old*___⌋ ⌊___*to drive*___⌋ a car.
                               too   +   adjective   +   infinitive

2. Susie doesn't want to go to the party because she is tired.

   → Susie is ⌊_____⌋ ⌊_____⌋ ⌊_____⌋ to the party.
                      too   +   adjective   +   infinitive

3. Robert is short. He can't touch the ceiling.

   → Robert is ⌊_____⌋ ⌊_____⌋ ⌊_____⌋ the ceiling.
                     too   +   adjective   +   infinitive

4. I couldn't finish my work because I was sleepy.

   → I was ⌊_____⌋ ⌊_____⌋ ⌊_____⌋ my work.
                  too   +   adjective   +   infinitive

5. Jackie is young. She can't get married.

   → Jackie is too . . . .

6. Sam didn't want to go to the zoo because he was busy.

   → Sam . . . .

7. I'm full. I can't eat another sandwich.

   → I . . . .

8. I don't want to clean up my apartment today. I'm lazy.

   → I . . . .

(a)	Bob can't lift the box because it is too heavy.		(a) and (b) have the same meaning.
(b)	The box is ***too heavy for Bob to lift***.		

		TOO +	ADJECTIVE +	*FOR (SOMEONE)* +	INFINITIVE
(c)	The box is	***too***	***heavy***	***for*** ***Bob***	***to lift***.
(d)	The dorm is	***too***	***noisy***	***for*** ***me***	***to study***.

■ **EXERCISE 18:** Make sentences with the same meaning by using ***too*** + ADJECTIVE + ***for*** *(someone)* + INFINITIVE.

1. Robert can't touch the ceiling because it's too high.

   → The ceiling is ⌊_ **too** _⌋ ⌊_ **high** _⌋ ⌊_ **for Robert** _⌋ ⌊_ **to touch** _⌋.
                     too + adjective + *for* (someone) + infinitive

2. I can't do the homework because it's too difficult.

   → The homework is ⌊_____⌋ ⌊_____⌋ ⌊_____⌋ ⌊_____⌋.
                     too + adjective + *for* (someone) + infinitive

3. Rosa can't drink this coffee because it's too hot.

   → This coffee is ⌊_____⌋ ⌊_____⌋ ⌊_____⌋ ⌊_____⌋.
                     too + adjective + *for* (someone) + infinitive

4. We can't go to the movie because it's too late.

   → It's ⌊_____⌋ ⌊_____⌋ ⌊_____⌋ ⌊_____⌋.
            too + adjective + *for* (someone) + infinitive

5. Ann can't carry that suitcase because it's too heavy.

   → That suitcase is too . . . .

6. I can't buy this book because it's too expensive.

   → This book . . . .

7. We can't go swimming because the weather is too cold.

   →

8. Mrs. Rivers can't swallow the pill. It's too big.

   →

■ **EXERCISE 19—ORAL (BOOKS CLOSED):** Answer *no* and explain why in a complete sentence that uses *too* and an INFINITIVE.

Example: The coffee is too hot. Can you drink it? Can (. . .) drink it?
Response: No. The coffee is too hot (for me) to drink. I think it's also too hot for (. . .) to drink.

1. *(This desk / A piano)* is heavy. Can you lift it? Can (. . .)?
2. (. . .)'s shoe is small. Can you wear it? Can (. . .) wear it?
3. (. . .)'s shoe is big. Can you wear it? Can (. . .) wear it?
4. Who wants to buy his or her own private airplane? How much does one cost? Can you buy one? Can (. . .) buy one?
5. Who is a parent? Has a son or daughter? How old? Can he/she walk/read/go to college/get a job/get married?
6. Antarctica is very, very cold. Do people live there?
7. There are many, many stars in the universe. Can we see all of them?
8. An elephant is a large animal. Can an elephant walk through that door?
9. The Sahara Desert is very dry. Do farmers grow (crops, rice, vegetables) there?
10. An apple is about the same size as my fist. Can you swallow a whole apple all at once? Can anyone swallow a whole apple all at once?

7-9 USING ADJECTIVE + *ENOUGH*

(a) Peggy can't go to school. She is too young. (b) Peggy can't go to school. She is not *old enough*.	(a) and (b) give the same meaning. Notice: *enough* follows an adjective.

(c) I can't hear the radio. It's not *loud enough*.
 (d) Bobby can read. He's *old enough*.
 (e) We can go swimming. The weather is *warm enough*.
	ADJECTIVE + ***ENOUGH***
	   old *enough*
	   loud *enough*
	   warm *enough*
	 Enough is pronounced "enuf."

■ **EXERCISE 20:** Complete the sentences. Use *too* or *enough*. Use the words in parentheses.

1. *(young, old)*   Susie can't go to school. She's ____*too young*____. She's not ____*old enough*____.

2. *(loud, soft)*   I can't hear the music. It's _____. It's not _____.

3. *(big, small)*   Jack is gaining weight. He can't wear his old coat. It's _____. It's not _____.

4. *(short, tall)*   Cindy can't reach the book on the top shelf. She's

_____ . She's not _____.

5. *(cold, hot)*   I don't want to finish my coffee because it's _____.

It's not _____.

6. *(weak, strong)*   Ron can't lift the heavy box. He's not _____.

He's _____.

7. *(sweet, sour)*   I don't want to finish eating this orange. It's _____.

It's not _____.

8. *(old, fresh)*   Don't buy that fruit. It's _____. It's not

_____.

9. *(young, old)*   Jimmy is an infant. He can't talk yet. He's not _____.

He's _____.

10. *(strong, weak)*   This coffee looks like dirty water. It's _____. It's

not _____.

11. *(big, small)*   I can put my dictionary in my shirt pocket. My pocket is

_____. It's not _____.

12. *(comfortable,*   I don't want to sit in that chair. It's _____.
     uncomfortable)

It's not _____.

13. *(wide, narrow,*   Anne and Sue can't carry the love
     large, small)   seat through the door. The door is

_____. The door

isn't _____. The

love seat is _____. The

love seat isn't _____.

14. *(warm, cold)*   We can go to the beach today. The weather is _____.

It's not _____.

■ **EXERCISE 21—ORAL (BOOKS CLOSED):** Answer the question *no* and explain why by using *enough*.

Example: Can you touch the ceiling?
Response: No, I'm not tall enough to touch the ceiling.

1. Can an elephant walk through that door?
2. Can ten-year-old children go to college?
3. Can you touch *(name of a student who is not close)* without standing up?
4. Can you put your grammar book in your shirt pocket?
5. Can a dog learn to read?
6. Can you eat *(four hamburgers)* right now?
7. Can you read a book by moonlight?
8. Can you understand every word an English-speaking TV newscaster says?
9. Can a turtle win a race with a rabbit?
10. *(Write something in very small letters on the board.)* Can you read these letters?
11. Can this room hold *(two hundred)* people?
12. Can you cut a piece of paper with your fingernail?

7-10 USING *ENOUGH* + NOUN AND *MORE* + NOUN

(a) I can't buy this book. I need **more money**. (b) I can't buy this book. I don't have **enough money**.	**more** = additional. **enough** = sufficient.

(c) I can't finish my work. I need some **more time**.
 (d) I can't finish my work. I don't have **enough time**.
	Notice: **more** comes in front of a noun.
	     MORE + *NOUN*
	     more *money*
	     more *time*
	 Notice: **enough** comes in front of a noun.★
	     ENOUGH + *NOUN*
	     enough *money*
	     enough *time*

★***Enough*** may also follow a noun: *I don't have money enough.* In everyday English, ***enough*** usually comes in front of a noun.

■ **EXERCISE 22:** Complete the sentences. Use your own words.

1. I can't _____ because I don't have enough money.

2. I can't _____ because I don't have enough time.

3. I couldn't _____ because I didn't have enough money.

4. I couldn't _____ because I didn't have enough time.

5. I don't want to _____ because I don't have enough time.

6. I would like to _____, but I can't because I don't have enough money.

■ **EXERCISE 23:** Complete the sentences. Use *more* or *enough*. Use the words in the list; use the plural form if necessary.

> ✔ bread   light   time
> desk   minute   vocabulary
> ✔ egg   sugar
> gas   tea

1. I'm hungry. I want to make a sandwich, but I can't. There isn't

_____ *enough bread* _____.

2. According to the cake recipe I need three eggs, but I have only one. I need two

_____ *more eggs* _____.

3. Ken isn't finished with his test. He needs ten _____.

4. I can't go skiing Saturday. I'm too busy. I don't have _____.

5. My tea isn't sweet enough. I need some _____.

6. There are fifteen students in the class, but there are only ten desks. We need five

_____.

7. I can't understand the front page of the newspaper because I don't know

_____.

8. It's too dark in here. I can't read my book. There isn't _____.

9. A: Do we have _____?
   B: No. We have to stop at a gas station.

10. A: Would you like _____?
    B: Yes, thank you. I'd like one more cup.

7-11 USING *ENOUGH* + INFINITIVE

(a) Peggy can go to school because she is old enough. ADJECTIVE + *ENOUGH* + INFINITIVE (b) Peggy is ***old*** ***enough*** ***to go*** to school.	(a) and (b) have the same meaning.
(c) I can't buy this book because I don't have enough money. *ENOUGH* + NOUN + INFINITIVE (d) I don't have ***enough*** ***money*** ***to buy*** this book.	(c) and (d) have the same meaning.

■ **EXERCISE 24:** Make sentences with the same meaning by using an INFINITIVE.

1. Ken can reach the top shelf because he's tall enough.
   → *Ken is tall enough to reach the top shelf.*

2. I can't finish my work because I don't have enough time.

3. Mustafa can buy a new car because he has enough money.

4. Johnny can't get married because he isn't old enough.

5. Mr. and Mrs. Forest can't feed their family because they don't earn enough money.

6. I can eat a horse. I'm hungry enough.★

7. Sally bought enough food. She can feed an army.

8. Did you finish your homework last night? Did you have enough time?

9. Can you buy a ticket to the show? Do you have enough money?

10. I can't understand this article in the newspaper because I don't know enough vocabulary.

★*I'm hungry enough to eat a horse* is an English idiom. The speaker is saying "I'm very hungry." The speaker does not really want to eat a horse.
    Other examples of idioms:
        I put my foot in my mouth. = I said something stupid. I said something to the wrong person at the wrong time.
        Watch your step. = Be careful.
        It's raining cats and dogs. = It's raining hard.
    Every language has idioms. They are common expressions that have special meanings.

■ **EXERCISE 25:** Complete the sentences. Use your own words.

1. I'm old enough to _____

2. I'm strong enough to _____

3. I'm not strong enough to _____

4. I'm not hungry enough to _____

5. I have enough money to _____

6. I don't have enough money to _____

7. I have enough time to _____

8. I don't have enough time to _____

9. I know enough English to _____

10. I don't know enough English to _____

■ **EXERCISE 26—ORAL (BOOKS CLOSED):** Answer *no* and explain why. Use *too* or *enough*.

Example: Is the weather perfect today?
Response: No, it's too cold. / No, it's not warm enough. / Etc.

1. I have a daughter. She's two years old. Can she go to school?
2. I'm making a noise (a very soft noise). Can you hear it?
3. Bobby is fifteen years old. He's in love. He wants to get married. Is that a good idea?
4. Can you put my briefcase/purse/etc. in your pants pocket/handbag/etc.?
5. Can you understand everything on the front page of a newspaper?
6. Can an elephant sit in that chair?
7. Do you like the weather (in this city) in the winter/summer?
8. Did you finish your homework last night?
9. Do you want to go on a picnic Saturday?
10. Would you like to eat your lunch on the floor of this room?
11. Can you buy a hotel?
12. Here's an arithmetic problem. You have three seconds to solve it (without a calculator). Multiply 673 by 897. Could you solve it in three seconds?

7-12 USING *BE ABLE TO*

PRESENT	(a) I **am able to touch** my toes. (b) I **can touch** my toes.	(a) and (b) have basically the same meaning.
FUTURE	(c) I **will be able to go** shopping tomorrow. (d) I **can go** shopping tomorrow.	(c) and (d) have basically the same meaning.
PAST	(e) I **wasn't able to finish** my homework last night. (f) I **couldn't finish** my homework last night.	(e) and (f) have basically the same meaning.

Will you be able to go shopping tomorrow?

■ **EXERCISE 27—ORAL:** Make sentences with the same meaning by using **be able to.** *It?*

Were you able to finish your homework last night?

1. I can be here tomorrow at ten o'clock.
   → *I'll (I will) be able to be here tomorrow at ten o'clock.*

2. Two students couldn't finish the test.
   → *Two students weren't able to finish the test.*

3. Mark is bilingual. He can speak two languages. *He is able to speak two languages*

4. Sue can get her own apartment next year.

5. Animals can't speak. *Animals are not able to speak.*

6. Can you touch your toes without bending your knees?

7. Jack couldn't describe the thief.

8. Could you do the homework?

9. I couldn't sleep last night because my apartment was too hot.

10. My roommate can speak four languages. He's multilingual. *many.*

11. I'm sorry that I couldn't call you last night.

12. I'm sorry, but I can't come to your party next week.

13. Can we take vacations on the moon in the 22nd century?

I will not be able to your party next week.
Will we be able to vacation

MOONLIGHT TOUR CO.

When I was very young I can't a

■ **EXERCISE 28:** Complete the sentences.

1. I wasn't able to _____ *call you* _____ last night because
   _____ *I was not home* _____.

2. We'll be able to _____ *go to Tibet* _____ in the 22nd century.

3. I'm sorry, but I won't be able to _____ *do some shopping* _____.

4. Birds are able to _____ *walk* _____.

5. My friend is multilingual. She's able to *speak many languages*

6. I'm bilingual. I'm able to *speak two languages*

7. The students weren't able to _____ *be* _____ in class
   yesterday because _____ *they were sick* _____.

8. Will you be able to _____ *come* _____ tomorrow?

9. _____ *The student* _____ wasn't able to _____ *do his homework* _____ because
   _____ *he wasn't in the class* _____.

10. _____ *Chun pay* _____ isn't able to _____ *sleep well* _____
    because _____ *he is thinking too much* _____.

11. _____ *L J* _____ won't be able to _____ *go outside* _____
    because _____ *The doors will be closed* _____.

7-13 POLITE QUESTIONS: *MAY I, COULD I,* AND *CAN I*

(a) **May I borrow** your pen? (b) **Could I borrow** your pen? (c) **Can I borrow** your pen?	(a), (b), and (c) have the same meaning: I want to borrow your pen. I am asking politely to borrow your pen.
(d) May I **please** borrow your pen? (e) Could I **please** borrow your pen? (f) Can I **please** borrow your pen?	**Please** is often used in polite questions.

TYPICAL RESPONSES
(g) **Yes, of course**.
(h) **Of course**.
(i) **Certainly**.
(j) **Sure**. (informal)★
(k) **No problem**. (informal)★
	TYPICAL CONVERSATION
	    A: *May I please borrow your pen?*
	    B: **Yes, of course**. *Here it is.*
	    A: *Thank you. / Thanks.*

★Informal English is typically used between friends and family members.

■ **EXERCISE 29:** Look at the pictures. Complete the dialogues by using *May I, Can I*, or *Could I* and typical responses.

■ **EXERCISE 30—ORAL (BOOKS CLOSED):** Ask and answer polite questions using *May I*, *Can I*, or *Could I*.

Example: (. . .) has a pencil. You want to borrow it.
STUDENT A: (. . .), may I (please) borrow your pencil?
STUDENT B: Certainly. Here it is.
STUDENT A: Thank you.

1. (. . .) has a dictionary. You want to borrow it.
2. (. . .) has a pen. You want to use it for a minute.
3. (. . .) has an eraser. You want to use it for a minute.
4. (. . .) has a pencil sharpener. You want to borrow it.
5. (. . .) has a book. You want to see it.
6. (. . .) has a dictionary. You want to see it.
7. You are at (. . .)'s home. You want to use the phone.
8. You are at (. . .)'s home. You want a glass of water.
9. You are at a restaurant. (. . .) is a waiter/waitress. You want to have a cup of coffee.
10. (. . .) is a waiter/waitress. You want to have the check.

7-14 POLITE QUESTIONS: *COULD YOU* AND *WOULD YOU*

(a) **Could you (please) open** the door? (b) **Would you (please) open** the door?	(a) and (b) have the same meaning: I want you to open the door. I am politely asking you to open the door.

TYPICAL RESPONSES
(c) **Yes, of course**.
(d) **Certainly**.
(e) **I'd be glad to**.
(f) **I'd be happy to**.
(g) **Sure**. (informal)
(h) **No problem**. (informal)
	TYPICAL CONVERSATION
	     A: *Could you please open the door?*
	     B: **I'd be glad to**.
	     A: *Thank you. / Thanks.*

Use the given expressions to complete the dialogues. Use **_Could you_** or **_Would you_** and give typical responses.

1. A: Excuse me, sir. _____

   B: _____

   A: _____

2. A: _____

   B: Excuse me? I didn't understand what you said.

   A: _____

   B: _____

■ **EXERCISE 32—ORAL (BOOKS CLOSED):** Ask and answer polite questions using *Could you* or *Would you*.

> *Example*: You want (. . .) to open the window.
> STUDENT A: (. . .), could you (please) open the window?
> STUDENT B: Certainly.
> STUDENT A: Thank you.

1. You want (. . .) to close the door.
2. You want (. . .) to turn on the light.
3. You want (. . .) to turn off the light.
4. You want (. . .) to pass you the salt and pepper.
5. You want (. . .) to hand you that book.
6. You want (. . .) to translate a word for you.
7. You want (. . .) to tell you the time.
8. You want (. . .) to open the window.
9. You want (. . .) to hold your books for a minute.
10. You want (. . .) to lend you *(an amount of money)*.

■ **EXERCISE 33—ORAL:** With a partner, make up a polite question that someone might typically ask in each situation. Share your dialogues with the rest of the class.
> STUDENT A: Ask a polite question.
> STUDENT B: Answer the question.

> *Example*: *Situation*: professor's office. Student A is a student. Student B is a professor.
> STUDENT A: *(Knock, knock).* May I come in?
> STUDENT B: Certainly. Come in. How are you today?
> STUDENT A: Fine, thanks.
>   OR:
> STUDENT A: Hello, Professor Alvarez. Could I talk to you for a few minutes? I have some questions about the last assignment.
> STUDENT B: Of course. Have a seat.
> STUDENT A: Thank you.

1. *Situation:* a restaurant. Student A is a customer. Student B is a waitress/waiter.
2. *Situation:* a classroom. Student A is a teacher. Student B is a student.
3. *Situation:* a kitchen. Student A is a visitor. Student B is at home.
4. *Situation:* a clothing store. Student A is the customer. Student B is a salesperson.
5. *Situation:* an apartment. Student A and B are roommates.
6. *Situation:* a car. Student A is a passenger. Student B is the driver.
7. *Situation:* an office. Student A is a boss. Student B is an employee.
8. *Situation:* a telephone conversation. Student B answers the phone. Student A wants to talk to *(someone)*.

7-15 IMPERATIVE SENTENCES

(a) "**Close** the door, Jimmy. It's cold outside." "Okay, Mom."	In (a): **Close the door** is an *imperative sentence*. The sentence means, "Jimmy, I want you to close the door. I am telling you to close the door."
(b) **Sit** down. (c) **Be** careful!	An imperative sentence uses the simple form of a verb (*close, sit, be, etc.*).
(d) **Don't open** the window. (e) **Don't be** late.	NEGATIVE: **don't** + *the simple form of a verb*
(f) ORDERS: **Stop**, thief! (g) DIRECTIONS: **Open** your books to page 24. (h) ADVICE: **Don't worry**. (i) REQUESTS: **Please close** the door.	Imperative sentence give orders, directions, and advice. With the addition of **please**, as in (i), imperative sentences are used to make polite requests.

■ **EXERCISE 34:** Underline the IMPERATIVE VERBS in the following dialogues.

1. CINDY: We're leaving.
   BETH: <u>Wait</u> for me!
   CINDY: <u>Hurry</u> up! We'll be late.
   BETH: Okay. Okay. I'm ready. Let's go.

2. MICHELLE: *(Knock, knock.)* May I come in?
   PROFESSOR: Certainly. Come in. Please have a seat.
   MICHELLE: Thanks.
   PROFESSOR: How can I help you?
   MICHELLE: I need to ask you a question about yesterday's lecture.
   PROFESSOR: Okay. What's the question?

3. MARY: We need to leave soon.
   IVAN: I'm ready.
   MARY: Don't forget your house key.
   IVAN: I have it.
   MARY: Okay.

4. TOM: What's the matter?
   JIM: I have the hiccups.
   TOM: Hold your breath.
   BOB: Drink some water.
   JOE: Breathe into a paper bag.
   KEN: Eat a piece of bread.
   JIM: It's okay. The hiccups are gone.

5. STUDENT: Do we have any homework for tomorrow?
   TEACHER: Yes. Read pages 24 through 36, and answer the questions on page 37, in writing.
   STUDENT: Is that all?
   TEACHER: Yes.

6. YUKO: How do I get to the post office from here?
   ERIC: Walk two blocks to 16th Avenue. Then turn right on Forest Street. Go two more blocks to Market Street and turn left. The post office is halfway down the street on the right-hand side.
   YUKO: Thanks.

7. ANDY: Bye, Mom. I'm going over to Billy's house.
   MOM: Wait a minute. Did you clean up your room?
   ANDY: I'll do it later.
   MOM: No. Do it now, before you leave.
   ANDY: Do I have to?
   MOM: Yes.
   ANDY: What do I have to do?
   MOM: Hang up your clothes. Make your bed. Put your books back on the shelf. Empty the wastepaper basket. Okay?
   ANDY: Okay.

8. HEIDI: Please close the window, Mike. It's a little chilly in here.
   MIKE: Okay. Is there anything else I can do for you before I leave?
   HEIDI: Could you turn off the light in the kitchen?
   MIKE: No problem. Anything else?
   HEIDI: Ummm, please hand me the remote control for the TV. It's over there.
   MIKE: Sure. Here.
   HEIDI: Thanks.
   MIKE: I'll stop by again tomorrow. Take care of yourself. Take good care of that broken leg.
   HEIDI: Don't worry. I will. Thanks again.

■ **EXERCISE 35:** Write an IMPERATIVE SENTENCE in the empty space above the speaker.

■ **EXERCISE 36—ORAL:** What are some typical IMPERATIVE SENTENCES you might hear in the given situations?

Example: (. . .) is your friend. He/She has a headache. What are some typical imperative sentences for this situation?

Responses: Take an aspirin.
Lie down and close your eyes for a little while.
Put a cold cloth across your forehead.
Take a hot bath and relax.
Etc.

1. You are the teacher of this class. You are assigning homework for tomorrow. What are some typical imperative sentences for this situation?
2. Your friend (. . .) has the hiccups. What are some typical imperative sentences for this situation?
3. (. . .) is your eight-year-old son/daughter. He/She is walking out the door to go to school. What are some typical imperative sentences for this situation?
4. (. . .) wants to improve his/her health. Tell him/her what to do and what not to do.
5. (. . .) is going to cook rice for the first time tonight. Tell him/her how to cook rice.
6. (. . .) is going to visit your country for the first time next month. Tell him/her what to do and what to see as a tourist in your country.

7-16 USING *TWO*, *TOO*, AND *TO*

			Two, too, and ***to*** have the same pronunciation.
TWO	(a)	I have ***two*** children.	In (a): ***two*** = a number.
TOO	(b)	Timmy is ***too*** young. He can't read.	In (b): ***too young*** = ***not old enough.***
	(c)	Ann saw the movie. I saw the movie ***too.***	In (c): ***too*** = ***also.***
TO	(d)	I talked ***to*** Jim.	In (d): ***to*** = a preposition.
	(e)	I want ***to*** watch television.	In (e): ***to*** = part of an infinitive.

■ **EXERCISE 37:** Complete the sentences. Use ***two***, ***too***, or ***to***.

1. I'd like a cup of coffee. Bob would like a cup _____*too*_____.

2. I had _____ cups of coffee yesterday.

3. I can't drink my coffee. It's _____ hot. The coffee is _____ hot for me _____ drink.

4. I talked _____ Jim. Jane wants _____ talk _____ Jim _____.

5. I walked _____ school today. Alex walked _____ school today _____.

6. I'm going _____ take the bus _____ school tomorrow.

7. Shh. I want _____ listen _____ the news broadcast.

8. I can't study. The music is _____ loud.

9. The weather is _____ cold for us _____ go _____ the beach.

10. I have _____ apples. Ken wants _____ have _____ apples _____.

7-17 MORE ABOUT PREPOSITIONS: *AT* AND *IN* FOR LOCATIONS

(a) Olga is *at* home. Ivan is *at* work. Yoko is *at* school.	In (a): *at* is used with *home, work,* and *school*.
(b) Sue is *in* bed. Tom is *in* class. Paul is *in* jail/prison. Mr. Lee is *in (the)* hospital.	In (b): *in* is used with *bed, class, jail/prison,* and *hospital*. NOTE: American English = *in the hospital*. British English = *in hospital*.
(c) Ahmed is *in* the kitchen.	In (c): *in* is used with rooms: *in the kitchen, in the classroom, in the hall, in my bedroom, etc.*
(d) David is *in* Mexico City.	In (d): *in* is used with cities, states/provinces, countries, and continents: *in Mexico City, in Florida, in Italy, in Asia, etc.*
(e) A: Where's Ivan? B: He isn't here. He's *at* the bank.	In (e): *at* is usually used with locations in a city: *at the post office, at the bank, at the library, at the bookstore, at the park, at the theater, at the restaurant, at the football stadium, etc.*
COMPARE (f) In Picture 2, Ivan is *in* the bank. He is not outside the bank.	In (f): A speaker uses *in* with a building only when it is important to say that someone is inside, not outside, the building. Usually a speaker uses *at* with a building. *in the bank* = inside the bank building.

Ivan is *at* the bank.

Ivan is *at* the bank.
Ivan is *in (inside)* the bank.

■ **EXERCISE 38:** Complete the sentences with *at* or *in*. In some sentences, both prepositions are correct.

1. A: Is Jennifer here?

   B: No, she's _____*at*_____ the bookstore.*

2. A: Where's Jack?

   B: He's _____*in*_____ his room.

3. When I was _____ work yesterday, I had an interesting telephone call.

4. Poor Anita. She's _____ the hospital again for more surgery.

5. Mr. Gow wasn't _____ class yesterday. He was _____ home. He wasn't feeling well.

6. Last year at this time, Eric was _____ Korea. This year he's _____ Spain.

7. A: Where's Donna?

   B: She's _____ New York. She's attending a conference.

8. There's a fire extinguisher _____ the hall.

9. The children are _____ home this morning. They aren't _____ school.

10. A: Where's Olga? I was supposed to meet her here at five.

    B: She's _____ the library. She's studying for a test.
    A: Oh. Maybe she forgot that she was supposed to meet me here.

11. A: Where's Robert?

    B: He's _____ the computer room.

12. A: Where's Fatima?

    B: She's _____ the supermarket.

13. We ate _____ a good restaurant last night. The food was delicious.

14. A thief broke the window of a jewelry store and stole some valuable jewelry. The

    police caught him. Now he's _____ jail. He's going to be _____ prison for a long time.

15. Singapore is _____ Asia.

16. We had a good time _____ the zoo yesterday.

_____

*ALSO CORRECT: *She's **in** the bookstore,* but only if the speaker wants to say that she is inside, not outside, the bookstore. Usually a speaker uses **at** with a building to identify someone's location.

17. There are thirty-seven desks _____ our classroom.

18. A: Where can I get some fresh tomatoes?

    B: _____ the market on Waterfront Street.

19. A: Here's your hotel key, Ms. Fox. You're _____ Room 609.
    B: Thank you. Where are the elevators?

20. A: Is Mike up?

    B: No, he's _____ bed.
    A: Well, it's time to get up. I'm going to wake him up. Hey, Mike! You can't sleep all day! Get up!
    C: Go away!

■ **EXERCISE 39—ORAL (BOOKS CLOSED):** Complete the sentence *"I was . . . yesterday"* by using the given word and the correct preposition, *at* or *in*.

Example: work
Response: I was at work yesterday.

1. class	7. work
2. the library	8. Room 206
3. *(name of a city)*	9. a hotel
4. home	10. *(name of a continent)*
5. this room	11. (. . .)'s living room
6. the bookstore	12. *(name of a building)*

■ **EXERCISE 40—ORAL (BOOKS CLOSED):** Ask and answer questions about location.
    STUDENT A: Begin the question with *"Where were you . . . . ?"*
    STUDENT B: Use *at* or *in* in the answer.

Example: yesterday afternoon
STUDENT A: Where were you yesterday afternoon?
STUDENT B: I was in class.

1. at nine o'clock last night
2. at two o'clock yesterday afternoon
3. after class yesterday
4. this morning at six o'clock
5. six weeks ago
6. five years ago
7. on your last vacation
8. when you were ten years old

■ **EXERCISE 41—REVIEW:** What *can* or *can't* the following people/animals/things do? Why or why not? Discuss the topics in small groups and report to the rest of the class.

> *Example:*   a tiger
> *Responses:*   A tiger can kill a water buffalo because a tiger is very strong and powerful.
>   A tiger can sleep in the shade of a tree all day if it wants to. It doesn't have a job, and it doesn't go to school.
>   A tiger can't speak (a human language). It's an animal.
>   A tiger can communicate with other tigers. Animals can talk to each other in their own languages.

1. the students in this class
2. small children
3. a monkey
4. *(name of a classmate)*
5. international students who live in *(name of this country)*
6. teenagers
7. people who live in *(name of this city)*
8. people who are illiterate
9. money
10. computers
11. *(name of the teacher of this class)*
12. *(name of the leader of this country or your country)*

■ **EXERCISE 42—REVIEW:** Choose the correct completion.

1. _____ play a musical instrument?
     A. Do you can   B. Can you   C. Do you be able to   D. Can you to

2. Jack was _____ sick to go to work yesterday morning. He stayed home.
     A. very   B. enough   C. too   D. too much

3. I was too sleepy _____ last night.
     A. to studying   B. for studying   C. to study   D. for study

4. *(Knock, knock.)* Hello? _____ come in? Thanks.
     A. Could I to   B. Will I   C. Can I to   D. May I

5. I don't know how _____ to the Palace Hotel from here.
     A. do I get   B. get   C. getting   D. to get

6. Gina _____ understand the speaker at the lecture last night.
     A. couldn't   B. might not   C. isn't able to   D. can't

7. In my life right now, I have _____ problems. I can't solve all of them.
     A. very much   B. too many   C. too much   D. very

8. I can't reach the eraser on my friend's desk. My arms aren't _____.
     A. long enough   B. too long   C. enough long   D. too much long

9. My uncle can't _____ English.
    A. to speak   B. speaking   C. speaks   D. speak

10. I'm sorry. I can't hear what you're saying. _____ speak a little louder?
    A. May you   B. Could you   C. Don't   D. Can

11. An encyclopedia is too difficult _____.
    A. for to read a child   C. for a child to read
    B. to read a child   D. to for a child read

12. Rosa works for a computer company _____ Taipei.
    A. on   B. at   C. in   D. to

■ EXERCISE 43—REVIEW: Correct the errors.

1. My brother wasn't able calling me last night.

2. Don't to interrupt. It's not polite.

3. May I please to borrow your dictionary? Thank you.

4. We will can go to the museum tomorrow afternoon.

5. We can't count all of the stars in the universe. There are to many.

6. The diamond ring was to buy too expensive for John.

7. Can you to stand on your head?

8. My son isn't enough old too go to school. He's only too years old.

9. I saw a beautiful vase at a store yesterday, but I couldn't bought it.

10. We have too many homeworks.

11. Closing the door please. Thank you.

12. Robert was to tired to go two his class at to o'clock.

■ **EXERCISE 44—REVIEW:** Complete the sentences. Use the words in parentheses. Use any appropriate verb form.

(1)   *Once upon a time there* (be) _____ *a mouse named Young Mouse. He lived near a river with his family and friends. Every day he and the other mice did the same things.*

(2)   *They* (hunt) _____ *for food and* (take) _____ *care of their*

(3)   *mouse holes. In the evening they* (listen) _____ *to stories around a fire. Young Mouse especially liked to listen to stories about the Far Away Land. He* (dream)

(4)   _____ *about the Far Away Land. It sounded wonderful. One day he*

(5)   (decide) _____ *to go there.*

YOUNG MOUSE: Goodbye, Old Mouse. I'm leaving now.

(6)   OLD MOUSE: Why *(you, leave)* _____? Where

(7)   *(you, go)* _____?

(8)   YOUNG MOUSE: I *(go)* _____ to a new and different place. I *(go)*

(9)   _____ to the Far Away Land.

(10)   OLD MOUSE: Why *(you, want)* _____ *(go)* _____ there?

(11)   YOUNG MOUSE: I *(want)* _____ *(experience)* _____

(12)   all of life. I *(need)* _____ *(learn)* _____ about everything.

(13)   OLD MOUSE: You *(can learn)* _____ many things if you *(stay)*

(14)   _____ here with us. Please *(stay)* _____ here with us.

(15)   YOUNG MOUSE: No, I *(can stay, not)* _____ here by the

(16)   river for the rest of my life. There *(be)* _____ too much to learn about in the world. I must go to the Far Away Land.

        OLD MOUSE: The trip to the Far Away Land is a long and dangerous journey. You *(have)*

(17)   _____ many problems before you *(get)* _____

(18)   there. You *(face)* _____ many dangers.

        YOUNG MOUSE: I understand that, but I need to find out about the Far Away Land.

(19)   Goodbye, Old Mouse. Goodbye, everyone! I *(may see, never)* _____

(20)   any of you again, but I *(try)* _____ to return from the
        Far Away Land someday. Goodbye!

        *So Young Mouse left to fulfill his dream of going to the Far Away Land. His first problem
was the river. At the river, he met a frog.*

(21)   MAGIC FROG: Hello, Young Mouse. I'm Magic Frog. *(you, have)* _____
        a problem right now?

(22)   YOUNG MOUSE: Yes. How *(I, can cross)* _____ this river?

(23)   I *(know, not)* _____ how to swim. If I

(24)   *(can cross, not)* _____ this

(25)   river, I *(be, not)* _____

        able to reach the Far Away Land.

(26)   MAGIC FROG: I *(help)* _____

        you to cross the river. I *(give)*

(27)   _____ you

        the power of my legs so you *(can jump)*

(28)   _____ across the river. I *(give, also)* _____
        you a new name. Your new name will be Jumping Mouse.

        JUMPING MOUSE: Thank you, Magic Frog.

        MAGIC FROG: You are a brave mouse, Jumping Mouse, and you have a good heart. If you

(29)   *(lose, not)* _____ hope, you *(reach)* _____
        the Far Away Land.

        *With his powerful new legs, Jumping Mouse jumped across the river. He traveled fast for
many days across a wide grassland. One day he met a buffalo. The buffalo was lying on the
ground.*

        JUMPING MOUSE: Hello, Buffalo. My name is Jumping Mouse. Why *(you, lie*)*

(30)   _____ on the ground? *(you, be)* _____ ill?

---

*The *-ing* form of *lie* is spelled *lying*.

(31)　BUFFALO: Yes. I *(can see, not)* _____. I *(drink)*

(32)　_____ some poisoned water, and now I *(be)* _____

(33)　blind. I *(die)* _____ soon because I *(can find, not)*

(34)　_____ food and water without my eyes.

(35)　JUMPING MOUSE: When I started my journey, Magic Frog *(give)* _____
　　　me her powerful legs so I could jump across the river. What *(I, can give)*

(36)　_____ you to help you? I know! I *(give)*

(37)　_____ you my sight so you can see to find food and water.

　　　BUFFALO: Are you really going to do that? Jumping Mouse, you are very kind! Ah! Yes,

(38)　I *(can see)* _____ again. Thank you! But now you

(39)　*(can see, not)* _____. How *(you, find)* _____

(40)　_____ the Far Away Land? I know. *(jump)*

(41)　_____ onto my back. I *(carry)* _____
　　　you across this land to the foot of the mountain.

　　　JUMPING MOUSE: Thank you, Buffalo.

　　　So Jumping Mouse found a way to reach the mountain. When they reached the mountain,
　　　Jumping Mouse and Buffalo parted.

(42)　BUFFALO: I don't live in the mountains, so I *(can go, not)* _____
　　　any farther.

(43)　JUMPING MOUSE: What *(I, do)* _____? I *(have)*

(44)　_____ powerful legs, but I can't see.

(45) BUFFALO: *(keep)* _____ your hope alive. You *(find)* _____
a way to reach the Far Away Land.

Jumping Mouse was very afraid. He didn't know what to do. Suddenly he heard a wolf.

(46) JUMPING MOUSE: Hello? Wolf? I *(can see, not)* _____ you,

(47) but I *(can hear)* _____ you.

(48) WOLF: Yes, Jumping Mouse. I'm here, but I *(can help, not)* _____

(49) you because I *(die★)* _____.

(50) JUMPING MOUSE: What's wrong? Why *(you, die)* _____?

(51) WOLF: I *(lose)* _____ my sense of smell many weeks ago, so now I

(52) *(can find, not)* _____ food. I *(starve)*

(53) _____ to death.

(54) JUMPING MOUSE: Oh, Wolf, I *(can help)* _____ you. I *(give)*

(55) _____ you my ability to smell.

(56) WOLF: Oh, thank you, Jumping Mouse. Yes, I *(can smell)* _____
again. Now I'll be able to find food. That is a wonderful gift! How *(I, can help)*

(57) _____ you?

(58) JUMPING MOUSE: I *(try)* _____ to get to the Far Away Land.

(59) I *(need)* _____ *(go)* _____ to the top of the mountain.

(60) WOLF: *(come)* _____ over here. I *(put)* _____

(61) you on my back and *(take)* _____ you to the top of the mountain.

_____
★The *-ing* form of *die* is spelled *dying*.

So Wolf carried Jumping Mouse to the top of the mountain. But then Wolf left. Jumping

(62)   *Mouse was all alone. He* (can see, not) _____

(63)   *and he* (can smell, not) _____ *, but he still had powerful legs.*

(64)   *He almost* (lose) _____ *hope. Then suddenly, he* (hear) _____ *Magic Frog.*

(65)   JUMPING MOUSE: Is that you, Magic Frog? Please *(help)* _____ me. I'm all alone and afraid.

(66)   MAGIC FROG: *(cry, not)* _____, Jumping Mouse. You have a

(67)   generous, open heart. You *(be, not)* _____ selfish. You help others. Your unselfishness caused you suffering during your journey, but you

(68)   *(lose, never)* _____ hope. Now you are in the Far

(69)   Away Land. *(jump)* _____, Jumping Mouse. *(use)* _____ your powerful legs to jump high in the air. Jump! Jump!

Jumping Mouse jumped as high as he could, up, up, up.
He reached his arms out to his sides and started to fly.
He felt strong and powerful.

JUMPING MOUSE: I can fly! I can fly! I *(fly)*

(70)   _____!

MAGIC FROG: Jumping Mouse, I am going to give you a new name. Now your name is Eagle!

So Jumping Mouse became the powerful Eagle and fulfilled his dream of reaching the Far Away Land and experiencing all that life has to offer.★

★This fable is based on a Native American story and has been adapted from *The Story of Jumping Mouse* by John Steptoe; © Lothrop, Lee & Shepard Books, 1984.

■ **EXERCISE 45:** In groups of six, create a play using the story of Jumping Mouse. There will be five characters in your play: Jumping Mouse, Old Mouse, Magic Frog, Buffalo, and Wolf. In addition, one person in the group will be the narrator. The narrator will tell the parts of the story that are in *italics* in Exercise 44. Rehearse your play in your group, and then present the play to the rest of the class.

7-18 MORE IRREGULAR VERBS

blow – blew	*keep – kept*
draw – drew	*know - knew*
fall – fell	*swim – swam*
feel – felt	*throw – threw*
grow – grew	*win – won*

■ **EXERCISE 46—ORAL (BOOKS CLOSED):** Practice using the IRREGULAR VERBS in the above list.

Example: *fall-fell* Rain falls. Leaves fall. Sometimes people fall. Yesterday I fell down. I hurt my knee. How did I hurt my knee yesterday?
Response: You fell (down).

1. *blow-blew*   The sun shines. Rain falls. Wind blows. Last week we had a storm. It rained hard, and the wind blew hard. Tell me about the storm last week.

2. *draw-drew*   I draw once a week in art class. Last week I drew a portrait of myself. What did I do in art class last week?

3. *feel-felt*   You can feel an object. You can also feel an emotion or a sensation. Sometimes I feel sleepy in class. I felt tired all day yesterday. How did I feel yesterday? How did you feel yesterday?

4. *fall-fell*   Sometimes I fall down. Yesterday I fell down. I felt bad when I fell down. What happened to me yesterday?

5. *grow-grew*   Trees grow. Flowers grow. Vegetables grow. Usually I grow vegetables in my garden, but last year I grew only flowers. What did I grow in my garden last year?

6. *keep-kept*   Now I keep my money in *(name of a local bank)*. Last year I kept my money in *(name of another local bank)*. Where did I keep my money last year?

7. *know-knew*   (. . .) knows a lot about English grammar. On the grammar test last week, s/he knew all the answers. What did (. . .) know last week?

8. *swim-swam*   I swim in *(name of a lake, sea, ocean, or local swimming pool)* every summer. I swam in *(name of a lake, sea, ocean, or local swimming pool)* last summer. What did I do last summer?

9. *throw-threw*   I can hand you this (piece of chalk) or I can throw it to you. I just
threw this (piece of chalk) to (. . .). What did I just do?

10. *win-won*   You can win a game or lose a game. Last weekend *(name of a local sports team)* won a game/match against *(name of another team)*. How did *(name of the local sports team)* do last weekend? Did they win or lose?

■ **EXERCISE 47:**   Complete the sentences. Use the past form of the verbs in the list.

blow	*grow*	*swim*
draw	*hurt*	*throw*
fall	*keep*	*win*
feel	*know*	

1. A: Did you enjoy your tennis game with Jackie?

   B: Yes, but I lost. Jackie _____.

2. A: How did you break your leg?

   B: I _____ down on the ice on the sidewalk.

3. A: Ouch!
   B: What's the matter?

   A: I _____ my finger.
   B: How?
   A: I pinched it in the door.

4. A: Did you give the box of candy to your girlfriend?

   B: No, I didn't. I _____ it and ate it myself.

5. A: That's a nice picture.

   B: I agree. Anna _____ it. She's a good artist.

6. A: Did you have a garden when you lived at home?

   B: Yes. I _____ vegetables and flowers.

7. A: Did you finish the test?

   B: No. I didn't have enough time. I _____ all of the answers but I ran out of time.

8. A: Did you have fun at the beach?

   B: Lots of fun. We sunbathed and _____ in the ocean.

9. A: I burned my finger.

   B: Did you put ice on it?

   A: No. I _____ on it.

10. A: What's the matter? You sound like you have a frog in your throat.

    B: I think I'm catching a cold. I _____ okay yesterday, but I don't feel very good today.

11. A: How did you break the window, Tommy?

    B: Well, I _____ a ball to Annie, but I missed Annie and hit the window instead.

■ **EXERCISE 48:** Complete the sentences. Use the past form of the verbs in the list.

begin	*fly*	*make*	*take*
break	*grow*	*meet*	*tell*
catch	*know*	*sing*	*throw*
cost	*leave*	*spend*	*wear*
fall	*lose*	*steal*	*win*

1. When I went to the airport yesterday, I _____ a taxi.

2. I _____ my winter jacket yesterday because the weather was cold.

3. Tom bought a new tie. It _____ a lot because it was a hand-painted silk tie.

4. Laurie doesn't feel good. She _____ a cold a couple of days ago.

5. Leo could read the story easily. The words in the story weren't new for him. He

   _____ the vocabulary in the story.

6. I know Ronald Sawyer. I _____ him at a party a couple of weeks ago.

7. My hometown is Ames, Iowa. I _____ up there.

8. I dropped my book. It _____ to the floor.

9. Ken couldn't get into his apartment because he _____ his keys.

10. We _____ a lot of money at the restaurant last night. The food was good, but expensive.

11. The baseball player _____ the ball to the catcher.

12. I wrote a check yesterday. I _____ a mistake on the check, so I tore it up and wrote another one.

13. Someone _____ my bicycle, so I called the police.

14. Maggie didn't tell a lie. She _____ the truth.

15. Rick _____ his arm when he fell on the ice.

16. We were late for the movie. It _____ at 7:00, but we didn't get there until 7:15.

17. We _____ songs at the party last night and had a good time.

18. I _____ to Chicago last week. The plane was only five minutes late.

19. My plane _____ at 6:03 and arrived at 8:45.

20. We played a soccer game yesterday. The other team _____. We lost.

CHAPTER **8**

Nouns, Adjectives, and Pronouns

■ **EXERCISE 1:** How are these words usually used, as NOUNS or ADJECTIVES? Use each word in a sentence.

1. busy   NOUN   (ADJ)
   → *I'm too busy to go to the zoo.*

2. computer   (NOUN)   ADJ
   → *Computers are machines.*

3. tall   NOUN   ADJ

4. apartment   NOUN   ADJ

5. Tom   NOUN   ADJ

6. intelligent   NOUN   ADJ

7. hand   NOUN   ADJ

8. good   NOUN   ADJ

9. monkey   NOUN   ADJ

10. young   NOUN   ADJ

11. music   NOUN   ADJ

12. expensive   NOUN   ADJ

13. grammar   NOUN   ADJ

8-1 MODIFYING NOUNS WITH ADJECTIVES AND NOUNS

(a) I bought an ADJECTIVE + NOUN ***expensive*** book.	Adjectives can modify nouns, as in (a). See Chart 4-2 for a list of common adjectives.
(b) I bought a NOUN + NOUN ***grammar*** book	Nouns can modify other nouns. In (b): *grammar* is a noun that is used as an adjective to modify another noun *(book)*.
(c) He works at a NOUN + NOUN ***shoe*** store. (d) INCORRECT: *He works at a shoes store.*	A noun that is used as an adjective is always in its singular form. In (c): the store sells shoes, but it is called a *shoe* (singular form) *store.*
(e) I bought an ADJECTIVE + NOUN + NOUN ***expensive*** ***grammar*** book. (f) INCORRECT: *I bought a grammar expensive book.*	Both an adjective and a noun can modify a noun; the adjective comes first, the noun second.

■ **EXERCISE 2:** Find the ADJECTIVES and identify the nouns they modify.

1. I drank some hot tea.

2. My grandmother is a wise woman.

3. English is not my native language.

4. The busy waitress poured coffee into the empty cup.

5. A young man carried the heavy suitcase for Fumiko.

6. I sat in an uncomfortable chair at the restaurant.

7. There is international news on the front page of the newspaper.

8. My uncle is a wonderful man.

■ **EXERCISE 3:** Find the NOUNS USED AS ADJECTIVES and identify the nouns they modify.

1. We sat at the kitchen table.

2. I bought some new CDs at the music store.

3. We met Jack at the train station.

4. Vegetable soup is nutritious.

5. The movie theater is next to the furniture store.

6. The waiter handed us a lunch menu.

7. The traffic light was red, so we stopped.

8. Ms. Bell gave me her business card.

■ **EXERCISE 4:** Complete the sentences. Use the information in the first part of the sentence. Use A NOUN THAT MODIFIES ANOTHER NOUN in the completion.

1. Vases that are used for flowers are called _____*flower vases.*_____

2. A cup that is used for coffee is called _____*a coffee cup.*_____

3. A story that appears in a newspaper is called _____

4. Rooms in hotels are called _____

5. Soup that is made of beans is called _____

6. A worker in an office is called _____

7. A room that contains computers is called _____

8. Seats on airplanes are called _____

9. A bench that is found in a park is called _____

10. A tag that gives the price of something is called _____

■ **EXERCISE 5:** Which noun in the list can be used with all three of the nouns used as modifiers? For example, in the first sentence below, the completion can be *a university education, a high school education,* and *a college education.*

class	*official*	*soup*
✔ *education*	*program*	*store*
keys	*race*	*tickets*
number	*room*	*trip*

1. Jane has a ⎰university⎱
    ⎰high school⎱ *education.* _____
    ⎱college⎰

2. We went to a ⎰furniture⎱
    ⎰shoe⎱ _____
    ⎱clothing⎰

3. I took a ⎰history⎱
    ⎰math⎱ _____
    ⎱science⎰

4. We watched a ⎰horse⎱
    ⎰car⎱ _____
    ⎱foot⎰

5. I talked to a ⎰government⎱
    ⎰city⎱ _____
    ⎱school⎰

6. Mom made some ⎰vegetable⎱
    ⎰bean⎱ _____
    ⎱chicken⎰

7. He told me about a ⎰radio⎱
    ⎰television⎱ _____
    ⎱computer⎰

8. We took a/an ⎰boat⎱
    ⎰bus⎱ _____
    ⎱airplane⎰

9. I couldn't find my ⎰car⎱
    ⎰house⎱ _____
    ⎱door⎰

10. What is your ⎰telephone⎱
    ⎰apartment⎱ _____
    ⎱license plate⎰

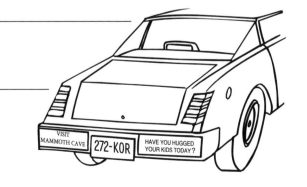

11. We bought some { theater / concert / airplane } _____

12. We visited Sue in her { hospital / hotel / dormitory } _____

■ **EXERCISE 6:** Each item lists two NOUNS and one ADJECTIVE. Put them in the correct order.

1. *homework*
   long
   assignment

   The teacher gave us a ___*long homework assignment.*___

2. *program*
   good
   television

   I watched a _____

3. *road*
   mountain
   dangerous

   We drove on a _____

4. *automobile*
   bad
   accident

   Janet was in a _____

5. *article*
   magazine
   interesting

   I read an _____

6. *delicious*
   vegetable
   soup

   Mrs. Green made some _____

7. *card*
   funny
   birthday

   My sister gave me a _____

8. *narrow*
   seats
   airplane

   People don't like to sit in _____

8-2 WORD ORDER OF ADJECTIVES

(a) a **large red** car (b) INCORRECT: *a red large car*	In (a): two adjectives *(large* and *red)* modify a noun *(car)*. Adjectives follow a particular order. In (a), an adjective describing **size** *(large)* comes before **color** *(red)* .
(c) a **beautiful young** woman (d) a **beautiful red** car (e) a **beautiful Greek** island	The adjective *beautiful* expresses an opinion. Opinion adjectives usually come before all other adjectives. In (c): opinion precedes age. In (d): opinion precedes color. In (e): opinion precedes nationality.
(f) OPINION ADJECTIVES *dangerous favorite important* *difficult good interesting* *dirty happy strong* *expensive honest wonderful*	There are many opinion adjectives. The words in (f) are examples of common opinion adjectives.

USUAL WORD ORDER OF ADJECTIVES

(1) **OPINION**	(2) **SIZE**	(3) **AGE**	(4) **COLOR**	(5) **NATIONALITY★**	(6) **MATERIAL**
beautiful	*large*	*young*	*red*	*Greek*	*metal*
delicious	*tall*	*old*	*blue*	*Chinese*	*glass*
kind	*little*	*middle-aged*	*black*	*Mexican*	*plastic*

(g) some **delicious Mexican** food (h) a **small glass** vase (i) a **kind old Chinese** man	A noun is usually modified by only one or two adjectives, although sometimes there are three.
(j) RARE: *a beautiful small old brown Greek metal coin*	It is very rare to find a long list of adjectives in front of a noun.

★NOTE: Adjectives that describe nationality are capitalized: **K**orean, **V**enezuelan, **S**audi **A**rabian, etc.

■ **EXERCISE 7:** Put the *italicized* words in the correct order.

1. *glass*   a _____*tall glass*_____ vase
   tall

2. *delicious*   some _____ food
   Thai

3. *red*   some _____ tomatoes
   small

4. *old*   some _____ cows
   big
   brown

5. *narrow*   a _____ road
   dirt

6. *young*   a _____ woman
   serious

7. *long*   _____ hair
   black
   beautiful

8. *Chinese*   a/an _____ work of art
   famous
   old

9. *leather*   a _____ belt
   brown
   thin

10. *wonderful*   a/an _____ story
   old
   Native American

■ **EXERCISE 8:**   Complete the sentences with words from the list below.

Asian	✔ *cotton*	*polite*
brick	*important*	*soft*
Canadian	*leather*	*unhappy*
coffee		

1. Jack is wearing a white _____*cotton*_____ shirt.

2. Hong Kong is an important _____ city.

3. I'm wearing some comfortable old _____ shoes.

4. Tommy was a/an _____ little boy when he broke his favorite toy.

5. Ann has a/an _____ wool blanket on her bed.

6. Our dorm is a tall red _____ building.

7. The computer is a/an _____ modern invention.

8. My nephew has good manners. He is always a/an _____ young man, especially to his elders.

9. Jack always carries a large blue _____ cup with him.

10. Ice hockey is a popular _____ sport.

■ **EXERCISE 9:** Add ADJECTIVES or NOUNS USED AS ADJECTIVES to the sentences below.

1. We had some hot _____ food.

2. My dog, Rover, is a/an _____ old dog.

3. We bought a blue _____ blanket.

4. Alice has _____ gold earrings.

5. Tom has short _____ hair.

6. Mr. Lee is a/an _____ young man.

7. Jack lives in a large _____ brick house.

8. I bought a big _____ suitcase.

9. Sally picked a/an _____ red flower.

10. Ali wore an old _____ shirt to the picnic.

■ **EXERCISE 10—ERROR ANALYSIS:**   Many, but not all, of the following sentences contain mistakes in the word order of modifiers. Find and correct the mistakes. Make changes in the use of **_a_** and **_an_** as necessary.

                                        an old wood
   1. Ms. Lane has ~~a wood old~~ desk in her office.

   2. She put the flowers in a blue glass vase. *(no change)*

   3. The Great Wall is a Chinese landmark famous.

   4. I read a newspaper article interesting this morning.

   5. Spiro gave me a wonderful small black Greek box as a birthday present.

   6. Alice reached down and put her hand in the mountain cold stream.

   7. Pizza is my favorite food Italian.

   8. There was a beautiful flower arrangement on the kitchen table.

   9. Jack usually wears brown old comfortable shoes leather.

 10. Gnats are black tiny insects.

 11. I used a box brown cardboard to mail a gift to my sister.

 12. Tony has a noisy electric fan in his bedroom window.

 13. James is a middle-aged handsome man with brown short hair.

 14. When Jane was on her last business trip, she had a cheap rental car, but she stayed in a room expensive hotel.

■ **EXERCISE 11—ORAL:** Practice modifying nouns.

STUDENT A: Your book is open. Say the words in each item. Don't let your intonation drop because Student B is going to finish the phrase.

STUDENT B: Your book is closed. Complete Student A's phrase with a noun. Respond as quickly as you can with the first noun that comes to mind.

Example: a dark . . .
STUDENT A: a dark
STUDENT B: night (room, building, day, cloud, etc.)

Example: some ripe . . .
STUDENT A: some ripe
STUDENT B: soup
STUDENT A: some ripe soup?? I don't think soup can be called ripe.
STUDENT B: Okay. How about "some ripe fruit"? OR: "some ripe bananas"?
STUDENT A: That's good. Some ripe fruit or some ripe bananas.

1. a kitchen . . .
2. a busy . . .
3. a public . . .
4. a true . . .
5. some expensive . . .
6. an interesting old . . .
7. an airplane . . .
8. a dangerous . . .
9. a beautiful Korean . . .
10. some delicious Mexican . . .

11. a birthday . . .
12. a computer . . .
13. a baby . . .
14. a soft . . .
15. an easy . . .
16. a government . . .
17. some hot . . .
18. a flower . . .
19. a bright . . .
20. some small round . . .

Switch roles.

21. a telephone . . .
22. a fast . . .
23. some comfortable . . .
24. a foreign . . .
25. a famous Italian . . .
26. a bus . . .
27. a history . . .
28. a rubber bicycle . . .
29. a hospital . . .
30. a movie . . .

31. some great old . . .
32. a television . . .
33. a very deep . . .
34. an office . . .
35. a gray wool . . .
36. an afternoon . . .
37. an empty . . .
38. a wonderful South American . . .
39. a bedroom . . .
40. a science . . .

(a)	Rita ate **all of** *the food* on her plate.	**All of**, **most of**, and **some of** express quantities.
(b)	Mike ate **most of** *his food.*	*all of* = 100%
(c)	Susie ate **some of** *her food.*	*most of* = a large part, but not all
		some of = a small or medium part
(d)	Matt ate **almost all of** his food.	*all of* = 100%
(e)	INCORRECT: *Matt ate almost of his food.*	*almost all of* = 95%–99%
		Almost is used with **all**; **all** cannot be omitted.

■ **EXERCISE 12:** Complete the sentences with *(almost) all of*, **most of**, or **some of**.

1. 2, 4, 6, 8: _____ *All of* _____ these numbers are even.

2. 1, 3, 5, 7: _____ these numbers are odd.

3. 1, 3, 4, 6, 7, 9: _____ these numbers are odd.

4. 1, 3, 4, 6, 7, 8: _____ these numbers are odd.

5. 1, 3, 4, 5, 7, 9: _____ these numbers are odd.

6. _____ the birds in Picture A are flying.

7. _____ the birds in Picture B are flying.

8. _____ the birds in Picture C are flying.

9. _____ the birds in Picture D are flying.

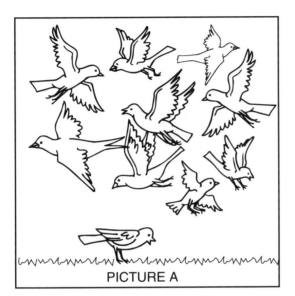

PICTURE A

PICTURE B

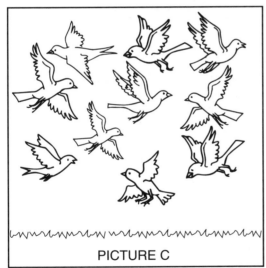

PICTURE C

PICTURE D

10. _____ the students in this class have dark hair.

11. _____ the students in this class are using pens rather than pencils to do this exercise.

12. _____ the students in this class wear glasses.

13. _____ the students in this class can speak English.

8-4 EXPRESSIONS OF QUANTITY: SUBJECT–VERB AGREEMENT

(a) *All of my* **work is** finished. (b) *All of my* **friends are** kind. (c) *Some of my* **homework is** finished. (d) *Some of my* **friends are** coming to my birthday party.	In (a): *all of* + **singular** noun + **singular** verb. In (b): *all of* + **plural** noun + **plural** verb. In (c): *some of* + **singular** noun + **singular** verb. In (d): *some of* + **plural** noun + **plural** verb.
	When a subject includes an expression of quantity, the verb agrees with the noun that immediately follows *of*.

COMMON EXPRESSIONS OF QUANTITY

all of	*most of*	*half of*
almost all of	*a lot of*	*some of*

■ **EXERCISE 13:** Choose the correct VERB.

1. All of that money _____*is*_____ mine.
    (is \ are)

2. All of the windows _____ open.
    (is \ are)

3. We saw one movie. Some of the movie _____ interesting.
    (was \ were)

4. We saw five movies. Some of the movies _____ interesting.
    (was \ were)

5. Half of the glasses _____ empty,
    (is \ are)

   and half of the glasses _____ full.
    (is \ are)

6. Half of the glass

   _____ empty.
    (is \ are)

IT'S HALF EMPTY.   IT'S HALF FULL.

Pessimist   Optimist

7. A lot of those words _____ new to me.
    (is \ are)

8. A lot of that vocabulary _____ new to me.
    (is \ are)

9. Almost all of the air in the city _____ polluted.
    (is \ are)

10. Almost all of the oceans in the world _____ polluted.
    (is \ are)

11. Most of the students _____ on time.
    (arrives \ arrive)

12. Most of our mail _____ in the morning.
    (arrives \ arrive)

8-5 EXPRESSIONS OF QUANTITY: *ONE OF, NONE OF*

ONE OF + PLURAL NOUN (a) Sam is **one** *of* my *friends*. (b) INCORRECT: *Sam is one of my friend.*	**One of** is followed by a specific **plural noun**, as in (a). It is INCORRECT to follow **one of** with a singular noun, as in (b).
ONE OF + PL. NOUN + SING. VERB (c) **One** *of* my *friends* **is** here. (d) INCORRECT: *One of my friends are here.*	When **one of** + *a plural noun* is the subject of a sentence, it is followed by a **singular verb**, as in (c): *ONE OF* + PLURAL NOUN + SINGULAR VERB.
(e) **None** *of the students* **was** late. (f) **None** *of the students* **were** late.	In (e): Not one of the students was late. 　　**none of** = **not one of** The verb following **none of** + *a plural noun* can be singular, as in (e), or plural, as in (f). Both are correct.*

*In very formal English, a singular verb is used after **none of** + *a plural noun*: *None of the students* **was** *late.* In everyday English, both singular and plural verbs are used.

■ **EXERCISE 14:** Make sentences from the given words and phrases.

1. One of my \ teacher \ be \ *(name of a teacher)*

   One of my teachers is Ms. Lopez.

2. *(name of a student)* \ be \ one of my \ classmate

   _____

3. one of my \ book \ be \ red

_____

4. one of my \ book \ have \ a green cover

_____

5. *(name of a place)* \ be \ one of my favorite \ place \ in the world

_____

6. one of the \ student \ in my class \ always come \ late

_____

7. *(name of a person)* \ be \ one of my best \ friend

_____

8. one of my \ friend \ live \ in *(name of a place)*

_____

9. *(title of a TV program)* \ be \ one of the best \ program \ on TV

_____

10. *(name of a person)* \ be \ one of the most famous \ people★ \ in the world

_____

11. one of my biggest \ problem \ be \ my inability to understand spoken English

_____

12. *(name of a newspaper)* \ be \ one of the \ leading newspaper \ in *(name of a city)*

_____

13. none of the \ student \ in my class \ speak \ *(name of a language)*

_____

14. none of the \ furniture \ in this room \ be \ soft and comfortable

_____

_____

★*People* is a plural noun even though it does not have a final **-s**.

■ **EXERCISE 15:** Complete the sentences with your own words.

1. One of my favorite _____ is _____.

2. _____ is one of the most interesting _____ in the world.

3. One of the _____ in my _____ is _____.

4. _____ is one of my best _____.

5. One of _____.

6. None of _____.

■ **EXERCISE 16:** Choose the correct VERB.

1. My grammar book _____*is*_____ red.
   (is \ are)

2. Some of my books _____ on my desk.
   (is \ are)

3. One of my books _____ blue and green.
   (is \ are)

4. My favorite colors _____ red and yellow.
   (is \ are)

5. Sue's favorite color _____ green.
   (is \ are)

BRAZIL

6. One of my favorite colors _____ red.
   (is \ are)

7. My best friends _____ in Brazil.
   (lives \ live)

8. One of my best friends _____ in Australia.
   (lives \ live)

9. Some of the students in my class _____ lap-top computers.
   (has \ have)

10. One of the students in Pablo's class _____ a mustache.
    (has \ have)

11. None of these letters _____ for you.
    (is \ are)

12. None of this mail _____ for you.
    (is \ are)

■ **EXERCISE 17:** Complete the sentences with *is* or *are*.

1. Some of the children's toys _____*are*_____ broken.

2. Most of my classmates _____ always on time for class.

3. One of my classmates _____ always late.

4. All of my friends _____ kind people.

5. One of my friends _____ Sam Brown.

6. Most of the rivers in the world _____ polluted.

7. Some of the Pacific Ocean _____ badly polluted.

8. Most of this page _____ white.

9. Most of the pages in this book _____ full of grammar exercises.

10. One of the pages in this book _____ the title page.

■ **EXERCISE 18—ORAL (BOOKS CLOSED):** Answer the questions in complete sentences. Use any expression of quantity (*all of, most of, some of, a lot of, one of, three of, etc.*).

Example: How many of the people in this room are wearing shoes?
Response: All of the people in this room are wearing shoes.

Example: How many of us are wearing blue jeans?
Response: Some of us are wearing blue jeans.

1. How many people in this room have (short) hair?
2. How many of the students in this class have red grammar books?
3. How many of us are sitting down?
4. How many of your classmates are from *(name of a country)*?
5. How many of the people in this room can speak (English)?
6. How many of the women in this room are wearing earrings? How many of the men?
7. What is one of your favorite TV programs?
8. How many of the people in this city are friendly?
9. Who is one of the most famous people in the world?
10. How many of the married women in your country work outside the home?

8-6 USING EVERY

(a) **Every student has** a book. (b) *All of the students* have books.	(a) and (b) have essentially the same meaning. In (a): **every** + **singular** noun + **singular** verb.
(c) INCORRECT: *Every of the students has a book.* (d) INCORRECT: *Every students have books.*	**Every** is not immediately followed by **of**. **Every** is immediately followed by a **singular** noun, NOT a plural noun.
(e) **Everyone has** a book. (f) **Everybody has** a book.	(e) and (f) have the same meaning. **Everyone** and **everybody** are followed by a **singular** verb.
(g) I looked at **everything** in the museum.	In (g): **everything** = each thing.
(h) **Everything is** okay.	In (h): **everything** is followed by a **singular** verb.

■ **EXERCISE 19:** Choose the correct completion.

1. All of the _____ *books* _____ on this desk _____ *are* _____ mine.
   (book \ books)   (is \ are)

2. Every _____ on this desk _____ mine.
   (book \ books)   (is \ are)

3. All of the _____ _____ here today.
   (student \ students)   (is \ are)

4. Every _____ _____ here today.
   (student \ students)   (is \ are)

5. Every _____ at my college _____ tests regularly.
   (teacher \ teachers)   (gives \ give)

6. All of the _____ at my college _____ a lot of tests.
   (teacher \ teachers)   (gives \ give)

7. Every _____ in my country _____ bedtime stories.
   (child \ children)   (likes \ like)

8. All of the _____ in my country _____ that story.
   (child \ children)   (knows \ know)

9. All of the _____ in this class _____ studying English.
   (person \ people)   (is \ are)

10. Everyone in this class _____ to learn English.
    (wants \ want)

11. _____ all of the _____ in this class speak English well?
    (Does \ Do)   (student \ students)

12. _____ every _____ in the world like to listen to music?
    (Does \ Do)   (person \ people)

13. _____ all of the _____ in the world enjoy dancing?
    (Does \ Do)   (person \ people)

14. _____ everybody in the world have enough to eat?
    (Does \ Do)

15. Every _____ in Sweden _____ a good transportation system.
          (city \ cities)   (has \ have)

■ **EXERCISE 20—ERROR ANALYSIS:**   Find and correct the errors.

   1. I work hard every days.

   2. I live in an apartment with one of my friend.

   3. We saw a pretty flowers garden in the park.

   4. Almost of the students are in class today.

   5. Every people in my class are studying English.

   6. All of the cities in North America has traffic problems.

   7. One of my books are green.

   8. Nadia drives a blue small car.

   9. Istanbul is one of my favorite city in the world.

  10. Every of students in the class have a grammar book.

  11. The work will take a long time. We can't finish every things today.

  12. Everybody in the world want peace.

8-7 POSSESSIVE NOUNS

		SINGULAR NOUN	POSSESSIVE NOUN	To show that a person possesses something, add an apostrophe (') and **-s** to a singular noun.
(a)	My *friend* has a car. My ***friend's*** car is blue.	*friend*	***friend's***	POSSESSIVE NOUN, SINGULAR noun + apostrophe (') + **-s**
(b)	The *student* has a book. The ***student's*** book is red.	*student*	***student's***	

		PLURAL NOUN	POSSESSIVE FORM	Add an apostrophe (') at the end of a plural noun (after the **-s**).
(c)	The *students* have books. The ***students'*** books are red.	*students*	***students'***	POSSESSIVE NOUN, PLURAL noun + **-s** + apostrophe (')
(d)	My *friends* have a car. My ***friends'*** car is blue.	*friends*	***friends'***	

■ **EXERCISE 21:** Add APOSTROPHES to the POSSESSIVE NOUNS.

    Jim's
 1. Jims ∧ last name is Smith.

 2. Bobs cat likes to sleep on the sofa.

 3. My teachers names are Ms. Rice and Mr. Molina.

 4. My mothers first name is Marika.

 5. My parents telephone number is 555-9876.

 6. My Uncle George is my fathers brother.

 7. Nicole is a girls name.

 8. Erica and Heidi are girls names.

 9. Do you like Toms shirt?

 10. Do you know Anitas brother?

 11. The teacher collected the students test papers at the end of the period.

12. Alexs friends visited him last night.

13. How long is an elephants trunk?

14. A monkeys hand looks like a human hand.

15. Monkeys hands have thumbs.

■ **EXERCISE 22:**   Complete the sentences. Use your classmates' names.

1. _____ hair is short and straight.

2. _____ grammar book is on her desk.

3. _____ last name is _____.

4. I don't know _____ address.

5. _____ eyes are gray.

6. _____ shirt is blue.

7. _____ briefcase is on the floor.

8. I need to borrow _____ dictionary.

9. Do you like _____ mustache?

10. Do you know _____ wife?

■ **EXERCISE 23—WRITTEN:** Write sentences about things your classmates possess.

   Example: Kim's book is on his desk. Anna's purse is brown. Pablo's shirt is green.

■ **EXERCISE 24:** Complete the sentences.

1. My husband's _____*brother*_____ is my brother-in-law.

2. My father's _____ is my uncle.

3. My mother's _____ is my grandmother.

4. My sister's _____ are my nieces and nephews.

5. My aunt's _____ is my mother.

6. My wife's _____ is my mother-in-law.

7. My brother's _____ is my sister-in-law.

8. My father's _____ and _____ are my grandparents.

9. My niece is my brother's _____.

10. My nephew is my sister's _____.

8-8 POSSESSIVE: IRREGULAR PLURAL NOUNS

(a) The **children's** *toys* are on the floor.	Irregular plural nouns *(children, men, women, people)* have an irregular plural possessive form. The apostrophe (') comes <u>before</u> the final **-s**.
(b) The store sells **men's** *clothing*.	
(c) That store sells **women's** *clothing*.	REGULAR PLURAL POSSESSIVE NOUN: *the* **students'** *books*
(d) I like to know about other **people's** *lives*.	IRREGULAR PLURAL POSSESSIVE NOUN: *the* **women's** *books*

■ **EXERCISE 25:** Complete the sentences with the correct possessive form of the NOUNS in *italics*.

1. *children*   That store sells _____*children's*_____ books.

2. *girl*   Mary is a _____ name.

3. *girls*   Mary and Sue are _____ names.

4. *women*   Mary and Sue are _____ names.

5. *uncle*   Robert is living at his _____ house.

6. *person*   A biography is the story of a _____ life.

7. *people*   Biographies are the stories of _____ lives.

8. *students*   _____ lives are busy.

9. *brother*   Do you know my _____ wife?

10. *brothers*   Do you know my _____ wives?

11. *wife*   My _____ parents live in California.

12. *dog*   My _____ name is Fido.

13. *dogs*   My _____ names are Fido and Rover.

14. *men*   Are Jim and Tom _____ names?

15. *man, woman* Chris can be a _____ nickname or a

       _____ nickname.

16. *children*   Our _____ school is near our house.

■ **EXERCISE 26:** Add appostrophes and final *-s* as necessary to make possessive nouns.

        Paul's

1. Someone stole Paul ∧ bicycle.

2. Do you know Yuko roommate?

3. Does that store sell women clothes?

4. My roommate desk is always a mess.

5. What is your parent new address?

6. I have my father nose.★

7. Where is Rosa apartment?

8. I can't remember all of my classmate names.

_____

★*I have my father's nose* = My nose looks like my father's nose; I inherited the shape of my nose from my father.

9. It's important to respect other people opinions.

10. My husband sister is visiting us this week.

11. Excuse me. Where is the men room?

12. That store sells children toys.

8-9 POSSESSIVE PRONOUNS: *MINE, YOURS, HIS, HERS, OURS, THEIRS*

		POSSESSIVE ADJECTIVE	POSSESSIVE PRONOUN	
(a)	This book belongs to me. It is *my* book. It is *mine*.	*my*	*mine*	A possessive adjective is used in front of a noun: *my* book.
(b)	That book belongs to you. It is *your* book. It is *yours.*	*your* *her* *his* *our* *their*	*yours* *hers* *his* *ours* *theirs*	A possessive pronoun is used alone, without a noun following it: *That book is **mine**.* INCORRECT: *That is mine book.*

■ **EXERCISE 27:** Complete the sentences. Use OBJECT PRONOUNS, POSSESSIVE ADJECTIVES, and POSSESSIVE PRONOUNS.

1. *I* own this book.

   This book belongs to ____me____.

   This is ____my____ book.

   This book is ____mine____.

2. *They* own these books.

   These books belong to _____.

   These are _____ books.

   These books are _____.

3. *You* own that book.

   That book belongs to _____.

   That is _____ book.

   That book is _____.

4. *She* owns this pen.

   This pen belongs to _____.

   This is _____ pen.

   This pen is _____.

5. *He* owns that pen.

   That pen belongs to _____.

   That is _____ pen.

   That pen is _____.

6. *We* own those books.

   Those books belong to _____.

   Those are _____ books.

   Those books are _____.

■ **EXERCISE 28:** Complete the sentences. Use the correct possessive form of the words in *italics*.

1. *I* a. This bookbag is _____mine_____.

 Sue b. That bookbag is _____Sue's_____.

 I c. _____My_____ bookbag is red.

 she d. _____Hers_____ is green.

2. *we* a. These books are _____.

 they b. Those books are _____.

 we c. _____ books are on the table.

 they d. _____ are on the desk.

3. *Tom* a. This raincoat is _____.

 Mary b. That raincoat is _____.

 he c. _____ is light brown.

 she d. _____ is light blue.

4. *I* a. This notebook is _____.

 you b. That one is _____.

 I c. _____ has _____ name on it.

 you d. _____ has _____ name on it.

5. *Jim* a. _____ apartment is on Pine Street.

 we b. _____ is on Main Street.

 he c. _____ apartment has three rooms.

 we d. _____ has four rooms.

6. *I* a. This is _____ pen.

 you b. That one is _____.

 I c. _____ is in _____ pocket.

 you d. _____ is on _____ desk.

7. *we*   a. _____ car is a Chevrolet.

  they   b. _____ is a Volkswagen.

  we   c. _____ gets 17 miles to the gallon.

  they   d. _____ car gets 30 miles to the gallon.

8. *Ann*   a. These books are _____.

  Paul   b. Those are _____.

  she   c. _____ are on _____ desk.

  he   d. _____ are on _____ desk.

■ **EXERCISE 29:** Choose the correct completion.

1. Is this _____*your*_____ pen?
           (your \ yours)

2. Please give this dictionary to Olga. It's _____.
                                            (her \ hers)

3. A: Don't forget _____ hat. Here.
                   (your \ yours)

   B: No, that's not _____ hat. _____ is green.
                     (my \ mine)   (My \ Mine)

4. A: Please take this wood carving as a gift from me. Here. It's _____.
                                                                 (your \ yours)

   B: Thank you. You're very thoughtful.

5. A: Isn't that the Smiths' car? That one over there. The blue one.

   B: No, that's not _____. _____ car is dark blue.
                     (their \ theirs)   (Their \ Theirs)

6. A: Jim and I really like _____ new apartment. It has lots of
                           (our \ ours)

   space. How do you like _____?
                          (your \ yours)

   B: _____ is small, but it's comfortable.
      (Our \ Ours)

7. A: Excuse me. Is this _____ umbrella?
                        (your \ yours)

   B: I don't have an umbrella. Ask Ken. Perhaps it is _____.
                                                       (him \ his)

8. A: When do _____ classes begin?
                            (your \ yours)

   B: September second. How about _____? When do
                                              (your \ yours)

       _____ begin?
       (your \ yours)

   A: _____ begin August twenty-ninth.
       (My \ Mine)

9. A: Maria, _____ spaghetti sauce is delicious!
                    (your\ yours)

   B: Thank you, but it's not as good as _____.
                                        (your \ yours)

   A: Oh, no. _____ is much better! It tastes just as good as Anna's.
                  (Your \ Yours)

   B: Do you like Anna's spaghetti sauce? I think _____ is too salty.
                                              (her\ hers)

   A: Maybe. _____ husband makes good spaghetti sauce too.
                  (My\ Mine)

       _____ is thick and rich.
       (His \ He)

   B: In truth, making spaghetti sauce is easy, but everyone's sauce is just a little different.

YOUR SPAGHETTI SAUCE
IS DELICIOUS, MARIA.

THANK YOU.

8-10 QUESTIONS WITH *WHOSE*

(a) ***Whose book*** is this? → Mine. → It's mine. → It's my book. (b) ***Whose books*** are these? → Rita's. → They're Rita's. → They're Rita's books.	***Whose*** asks about possession. ***Whose*** is often used with a noun (e.g., *whose book)*, as in (a) and (b).
(c) ***Whose*** is this? *(The speaker is pointing to a book.)* (d) ***Whose*** are these? *(The speaker is pointing to some books.)*	***Whose*** can be used without a noun if the meaning is clear, as in (c) and (d).

WHOSE IS THIS? THERE'S NO NAME ON IT. WHO'S THE ARTIST?

■ **EXERCISE 30:** Choose the correct completion.

1. Whose watch ____*is*____ ____*this*____?
   (is \ are)   (this \ these)

2. Whose glasses _____ _____?
   (is \ are)   (that \ those)

3. Whose keys _____ _____?
   (is \ are)   (this \ these)

4. Whose hat _____ _____?
   (is \ are)   (that \ those)

5. Whose shoes _____ _____?
   (is \ are)   (that \ those)

6. Whose handbag _____ _____?
   (is \ are)   (this \ these)

■ **EXERCISE 31:** Point to or touch something in the classroom that belongs to someone and ask a question with **whose**.

> *Example:*   (Student A points to or touches a grammar book.)
> STUDENT A: Whose book is this?
> STUDENT B: It's mine. / Mine. / It's my book.
> STUDENT A: Whose book is that?
> STUDENT B: It's Po's. / Po's. / It's Po's book.

8-11 SUMMARY: USES OF THE APOSTROPHE

(a) ***I'm*** happy. (INCORRECT: *I'am happy.*) ***She's*** happy. ***We're*** happy. (b) ***Tom's*** happy.	USES OF THE APOSTROPHE • With contractions of pronouns and ***am, is,*** and ***are***. See Chart 1-4. • With contractions of nouns and ***is***. In (b), ***Tom's*** = *Tom is.* *
(c) ***That's*** my notebook.	• With the contraction of ***that*** and ***is***.
(d) ***There's*** a book on the table. ***There're*** some books on the table.	• With the contractions of ***there*** and ***is/are***.
(e) ***What's*** this? ***Where's*** Anna?	• With contractions of some question words and ***is***.
(f) ***Who's*** that? → It's *Mike.* ***Whose*** is that? → It's *Mike's.*	COMPARE In (f): ***Who's*** = *who is.* In (g): ***Whose*** = a question word that asks about possession. It has NO apostrophe.
(h) Tina ***isn't*** here.	• With negative contractions: ***isn't, aren't, wasn't, weren't, doesn't, don't, won't, can't***.
(i) ***Tom's*** hair is brown. (j) My ***parents'*** house is white. (k) This pen belongs to Ann. It is ***hers***. (l) INCORRECT: *It is her's.*	• With possessive nouns, as in (i) and (j). See Charts 8-7 and 8-8. Apostrophes are NOT used with possessive pronouns. In (l): *hers* with an apostrophe (*her's*) is NEVER correct.
(m) ***It's*** sunny today. (n) I'm studying about India. I'm interested in ***its*** history. (o) INCORRECT: *I'm interested in it's history.*	COMPARE: In (m): ***it's*** = *it is.* In (n): ***its*** = a possessive adjective: ***its*** history = ***India's*** *history.* A possessive adjective has NO apostrophe.

*Nouns are regularly contracted with *is* in spoken English. In written English, contractions of a noun and *is* (e.g., *Tom's happy*) are found in informal English (for example, in a letter to a friend), but not in formal English (for example, an academic paper). In general, verb contractions (*I'm, you're, isn't, there's,* etc.) are found in informal English, but are not used in very formal English.

■ **EXERCISE 32:** Add apostrophes where necessary.

1. Thats Anns book. → *That's Ann's book.*

2. That book is hers. → *(no change)*

3. Jims car is small.

4. Jims in New York this week.

5. Hes visiting his brother.

6. Im a little hungry this morning.

7. Tonys my neighbor.

8. Tonys apartment is next to mine.

9. Whos that woman?

10. Shes Bobs wife.

11. Whose book is that?

12. Is it yours?

13. Its Ginas book.

14. Wheres your dictionary?

15. Amy wont go to the movie with us.   She doesnt have enough money.

16. Paris is a popular tourist destination. Its most famous attraction is the Eiffel Tower.

Its most famous building is the Louvre Museum. Its also famous for its night life.

■ **EXERCISE 33:** Add apostrophes where necessary.

Yoko's
1. Yokos ∧ last name is Yakamoto.

2. Yokos a student in my English class.

3. Pablo is a student. Hes in my class. His last name is Alvarez.

4. Pablos full name is Pablo Alvarez.

5. Youre a student. Your name is Ali.

6. Im a student. I am in Mr. Lees English class.

7. Mary and Anita have purses. Marys purse is black. Anitas purse is brown.

8. Marys in class today. Anitas at home.

9. Whose books are these? This book is mine. Thats yours.

10. Whats wrong? Whats happening? Whos that man? Wheres he going?

11. Im looking at a book. Its a grammar book. Its cover is red. Its on my desk. Its

    open. Its title is *Basic English Grammar*.

12. Theres a bird in the tree. Its black and red. Its chest is red. Its wings, tail, and back

    are black. Its sitting on a branch.

13. People admire the tiger for its beauty and strength. Its a magnificent animal.

    Unfortunately, its survival as a species is in doubt. Its an endangered species.

    Therere very few tigers in the world today.

(a) NOUN | **_Birds_** | fly. | subject verb	NOUNS ARE USED AS: • subjects of a sentence, as in (a).
(b) NOUN | Ken | opened | _the **door.**_ | subject verb object	• objects of a verb, as in (b).
(c) NOUN | Birds | fly | in | _the **sky**_. | subject verb prep. object of prep.	• objects of a preposition, as in (c).
(d) NOUN | Yoko | is | _a **student.**_ | subject _be_ noun complement	• noun complements* after **_be_**, as in (d).
(e) NOUN + NOUN I don't like **_winter_** _weather._	• modifiers of other nouns, as in (e).
(f) NOUN + NOUN I like **_Jim's_** _hat._	• possessives, as in (f).

*A _complement_ is a word that <u>completes</u> a sentence or a thought.

■ **EXERCISE 34:** Write the sentences that fit the grammatical descriptions. Circle the NOUNS.

       a. A kangaroo is an animal.
       b. My wallet is in my pocket.

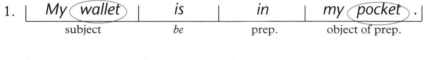

1. \| My (wallet) \| is \| in \| my (pocket) . \|
      subject   _be_   prep.   object of prep.

2. subject   _be_   noun complement

       c. Jason works in an office.
       d. Karen held the baby in her arms.
       e. Restaurants serve food.

3. subject   verb   object

4. subject   verb   prep.   object of prep.

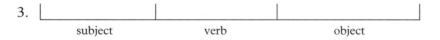

5. subject   verb   object   prep.   object of prep.

f. Korea is in Asia.
g. Korea is a peninsula.

6.

subject	*be*	prep.	object of prep.

7.

subject	*be*	noun complement

h. Children play with toys.
i. Monkeys eat fruit.
j. Jack tied a string around the package.

8.

subject	verb	object

9.

subject	verb	prep.	object of prep.

10.

subject	verb	object	prep.	object of prep.

8-13 CONNECTED NOUNS: NOUN + AND/OR + NOUN

NOUN + *and* + NOUN
(a) | **Birds** *and* **airplanes** | fly. |
     subject   verb
 	
                  NOUN + *and* + NOUN
(b) | Ken | opened | *the **door** and the **window.*** |
  subject   verb   object
 	
            NOUN + NOUN + *and* + NOUN
(c) | I | have | *a **book**, a **pen**, and a **pencil.*** |
 subject verb   object
	And can connect two or more nouns.
	In (a): the subject = two nouns.
	In (b): the object = two nouns.
	In (c): the object = three nouns.
	Three (or more) nouns are separated by commas, as in (c). Two nouns, as in (a) and (b), are NOT separated by commas.

NOUN + *or* + NOUN (d) I'd like *some coffee* **or** *some tea.*	***Or*** can also connect two nouns, as in (d).

■ **EXERCISE 35:** Find the CONNECTED NOUNS and discuss how they are used.

1. You bought apples and bananas.
   → *apples and bananas = connected nouns, used as the object of the verb "bought"*

2. I bought apples, bananas, and oranges.

3. Jack and Olga bought bananas.

4. Julia wants apples or bananas.

5. Julia is at the market with Jack and Olga.

6. Tennis and golf are popular sports.

7. Tokyo has excellent museums and libraries.

8. A tree has a trunk, branches, leaves, and roots.

9. Automobiles, trains, and trucks are kinds of vehicles.

10. I'll have some soup or a sandwich for lunch.

■ **EXERCISE 36:** Add commas where necessary.

1. Ants bees and mosquitoes are insects.
   → *Ants, bees, and mosquitoes are insects.*★

2. Ants and bees are insects. *(no change)*

3. Bears tigers and elephants are animals.

4. Bears and tigers are animals.

5. I bought some rice fruit and vegetables at the market.

6. I bought some rice and fruit at the market.

7. The three countries in North America are Canada the United States and Mexico.

8. I read a lot of newspapers and magazines.

9. I had some soup and a sandwich for lunch.

10. Shelley had some soup a salad and a sandwich for lunch.

11. My favorite things in life are sunny days music good friends and books.

12. What do birds butterflies and airplanes have in common?

■ **EXERCISE 37:** Find the NOUNS. Discuss how they are used.

1. A turtle is a reptile.
   → *turtle = a noun, used as the subject of the sentence.*
   → *reptile = a noun, used as a complement after "be."*

2. A turtle has a hard shell.

3. A turtle pulls its head, legs, and tail into its shell.

4. Some turtles spend almost all of their lives in water.

5. Some turtles live on land for their entire lives.

6. Turtles don't have teeth, but they have powerful jaws.

★In a series of connected nouns, the comma immediately before ***and*** is optional.
ALSO CORRECT: *Ants, bees and mosquitoes are insects.*

7. Turtles bury their eggs in sand or mud.

8. Baby turtles face many dangers.

9. Birds and fish eat baby turtles.

10. Some green sea turtles live for 100 years.

11. Turtles face many dangers from people.

12. People destroy turtles' natural homes.

13. People replace beaches, forests, and other natural areas with towns and farms.

14. People poison natural areas with pollution.

15. Many species of turtles face extinction.

8-14 SUMMARY: USES OF ADJECTIVES

(a) I bought some **beautiful** **flowers**. ADJECTIVE + NOUN	Adjectives describe nouns; they give information about nouns. See Chart 4-2 for a list of common adjectives. Adjectives can come in front of nouns, as in (a).
(b) The flowers **were** **beautiful**. BE + ADJECTIVE	Adjectives can follow **be**, as in (b). The adjective describes the subject of the sentence. See Chart 1-6.
LINKING VERB + ADJECTIVE (c) The flowers **looked** **beautiful**. (d) The flowers **smelled** **good**. (e) I **feel** **good**. (f) Candy **tastes** **sweet**. (g) That book **sounds** **interesting**.	Adjectives can follow a few other verbs. These verbs are called "linking verbs." The adjective describes the subject of the sentence. Common linking verbs are: *look, smell, feel, taste,* and *sound.*

■ **EXERCISE 38:** Find the ADJECTIVES and discuss ways adjectives are used.

1. The sun is bright today.
   → *bright = an adjective. It follows "be" and describes the subject of the sentence, "sun."*

2. I drank some cold water.

3. My dog's nose is cold.

4. Ice feels cold.

5. This exercise looks easy.

6. Our teacher gives easy tests.

7. English grammar is easy.

8. Lemons taste sour.

9. What's the matter? You look unhappy.

10. I'm sad.

11. Who is your favorite author?

12. What's the matter? You sound angry.

13. Ummm. These flowers smell wonderful!

14. That chair looks soft and comfortable.

15. Mr. White is a good history teacher.

■ **EXERCISE 39—ORAL:** Practice using linking verbs.

PART I: Do any of the following ADJECTIVES describe how you feel today?

1. good	5. sleepy	9. happy
2. fine	6. tired	10. calm
3. terrible	7. lazy	11. sick
4. terrific	8. nervous	12. old

PART II: Name things that . . .

13. taste good	17. taste sour
14. taste terrible	18. smell good
15. taste delicious	19. smell bad
16. taste sweet	20. smell wonderful

PART III: Name something in this room that looks . . .

21. clean	25. expensive
22. dirty	26. comfortable
23. new	27. messy
24. old	28. familiar

■ **EXERCISE 40—ORAL:** Describe how your classmates look.

STUDENT A: Choose one of the emotions listed below. Show that emotion through expressions on your face and through your actions. Don't tell anyone which emotion you're trying to show.

STUDENT B: Describe how Student A looks. Use the linking verb *look* and an adjective.

1. angry	5. busy
2. sad / unhappy	6. comfortable
3. happy	7. surprised
4. tired / sleepy	8. nervous

■ **EXERCISE 41:** Use any possible completions for the following sentences. Use the words in the list or your own words.

easy	*good / terrific / wonderful / great*	*interesting*
hard / difficult	*terrible / awful*	*tired / sleepy*

1. Rosa told me about a new book. I want to read it. It sounds ___*interesting /*___
   ___*good / terrific*___.

2. Karen learned how to make paper flowers. She told me how to do it. It sounds
   _____.

3. There's a new play at the community theater. I read a review of it in the newspaper. I'd like to see it. It sounds _____.

4. Professor Wilson is going to lecture on the problems of overpopulation tomorrow evening. I think I'll go. It sounds _____.

5. Chris explained how to fix a flat tire. I think I can do it. It sounds

_____.

6. Shelley didn't finish her dinner because it didn't taste _____.

7. What's for dinner? Something smells _____. Ummm! What is it?

8. Amy didn't get any sleep last night because she studied all night for a test. Today she

looks _____.

9. Ymmmm! This dessert tastes _____. What is it?

10. A: What's the matter? Do you feel okay?

    B: No. I feel _____. I think I'm getting a cold.

11. A: Do you like my new dress, darling?

    B: You look _____, honey.

12. A: Pyew!* Something smells _____! Do you smell it too?
    B: I sure do. It's the garbage in the alley.

■ **EXERCISE 42:** Work in pairs or small groups. In a given time limit (e.g., fifteen seconds, thirty seconds, a minute), think of as many ADJECTIVES or NOUNS USED AS ADJECTIVES as you can that can be used to describe the nouns. Make a list.

Example: car
Response: big, little, fast, slow, comfortable, small, large, old, new, used, noisy, quiet, foreign, electric, antique, police, etc.

1. weather   5. country
2. animal   6. person
3. food   7. river
4. movie   8. student

---

*Pyew is sometimes said "p.u." Both *Pyew* and *p.u.* mean that something smells very bad.

8-15 SUMMARY: PERSONAL PRONOUNS

	SUBJECT PRONOUNS	OBJECT PRONOUNS	POSSESSIVE PRONOUNS	POSSESSIVE ADJECTIVES
SINGULAR	*I*	*me*	*mine*	*my* name(s)
	you	*you*	*yours*	*your* name(s)
	she	*her*	*hers*	*her* name(s)
	he	*him*	*his*	*his* name(s)
	it	*it*		*its* name(s)
PLURAL	*we*	*us*	*ours*	*our* name(s)
	you	*you*	*yours*	*your* name(s)
	they	*them*	*theirs*	*their* name(s)

(a) ***We*** saw an accident.	Personal pronouns are used as:
(b) Anna saw ***it*** too.	• subjects, as in (a);
(c) I have my pen. Sue has ***hers***.	• objects, as in (b);
(d) ***Her*** pen is blue.	• OR to show possession, as in (c) and (d).

(e) I have a book. ***It*** is on my desk.	Use a singular pronoun to refer to a singular noun. In (e): *book* and *it* are both singular.
(f) I have some books. ***They*** are on my desk.	Use a plural pronoun to refer to a plural noun. In (f): *books* and *they* are both plural.

■ **EXERCISE 43:** PRONOUN review. Find and correct the errors in pronoun usage.

Dear Heidi,

(1)   Everything is going fine. I like ~~mine~~ *my* new apartment very much. Its large and

(2)   comfortable. I like me roommate too. Him name is Alberto. You will meet them

(3)   when your visit I next month. His from Colombia. His studying English too. Were

(4)   classmates. We were classmates last semester too.

(5)   We share the rent and the utility bills, but us don't share the telephone bill.

(6)   He pays for his's calls and my pay for my. He's telephone bill is very high because

(7)   he has a girlfriend in Colombia. He calls she often. Sometimes her calls he. Them

(8)   talk on the phone a lot.

(9)   Ours neighbors are Mr. and Mrs. Black. Their very nice. We talk to it often.

(10)   Ours apartment is next to their. Theirs have a three-year-old* daughter. Shes

(11)   really cute. Hers name is Joy. Them also have a cat. Its black and white. Its eyes

---

*NOTE: When a person's age is used as an adjective in front of a noun, the word *year* is singular (NOT plural) and hyphens (-) are used: *a three-year-old daughter.*
    INCORRECT: *They have a three years old daughter.*
    CORRECT: *They have a three-year-old daughter.* OR: *Their daughter is three years old.*

(12)   are yellow. Its name is Whiskers. Its a friendly cat. Sometimes they're cat leaves a

(13)   dead mouse outside ours door.

(14)   I'am looking forward to you're visit.

Love, Carl

8-16 INDIRECT OBJECTS

(a) I wrote │ *a letter* │ **to Alex**. │ direct object INDIRECT object	Some verbs are followed by two objects: a direct object and an indirect object. (a) and (b) have the same meaning. The preposition **to** is NOT used when the indirect object is first and the direct object is second.
(a) I wrote │ **Alex** │ │ a letter. │ INDIRECT object direct object	
(c) INCORRECT: *I wrote to Alex a letter.*	
(d) DIRECT OBJECT What did you write? → A letter.	A direct object answers the question *What?*
(e) INDIRECT OBJECT Who(m) did you write a letter to? → Alex.	An indirect object answers the question *Who(m)?*
(f) —Did you write these letters to Alex? —Yes, I did. I wrote **them to him**.	When the direct object is a pronoun (e.g., *them*), it must precede the indirect object, as in (f).
(g) INCORRECT: *I wrote him them.*	

VERBS FOLLOWED BY INDIRECT OBJECTS INTRODUCED BY **TO**

give	*send*
hand	*show*
lend	*tell*
pass	*write*

■ **EXERCISE 44:**   Use the given words to complete the grammar descriptions.

  1. my pen \ Heidi \ I gave

a. | *I gave* | *my pen* | *to Heidi.* |
   subject and verb | direct object | INDIRECT object

b. | *I gave* | *Heidi* | *my pen.* |
   subject and verb | INDIRECT object | direct object

  2. I wrote \ Kim \ a letter

a. | | | |
   subject and verb | direct object | INDIRECT object

b. | | | |
   subject and verb | INDIRECT object | direct object

3. Jack handed \ a book \ Hiroki

a. |_____|_____|_____|
   subject and verb   direct object   INDIRECT object

b. |_____|_____|_____|
   subject and verb   INDIRECT object   direct object

4. Stacy \ I passed \ the salt

a. |_____|_____|_____|
   subject and verb   direct object   INDIRECT object

b. |_____|_____|_____|
   subject and verb   INDIRECT object   direct object

5. I lent \ my car \ Tom

a. |_____|_____|_____|
   subject and verb   direct object   INDIRECT object

b. |_____|_____|_____|
   subject and verb   INDIRECT object   direct object

6. Alice \ a postcard \ I sent

a. |_____|_____|_____|
   subject and verb   direct object   INDIRECT object

b. |_____|_____|_____|
   subject and verb   INDIRECT object   direct object

7. Ann told \ a story \ us

a. |_____|_____|_____|
   subject and verb   direct object   INDIRECT object

b. |_____|_____|_____|
   subject and verb   INDIRECT object   direct object

8. us \ a picture \ Jack showed

a. |_____|_____|_____|
   subject and verb   direct object   INDIRECT object

b. |_____|_____|_____|
   subject and verb   INDIRECT object   direct object

■ **EXERCISE 45—ORAL:**   Change the position of the INDIRECT OBJECT in the following sentences. Be sure to omit **to**.

    1. I gave my pen to Alex.
       → *I gave Alex my pen.*
    2. Please hand that book to me.
    3. Rosa wrote a letter to her brother.
    4. I gave a birthday present to Ahmed.
    5. Please tell a story to us.
    6. Did you send a package to your parents?
    7. Mr. Hong showed a photograph of his wife to me.
    8. Would you lend your camera to me?

■ **EXERCISE 46—ORAL (BOOKS CLOSED):**   Change the position of the INDIRECT OBJECT.

    Example: You gave your book to (. . .). What did you do?
    Response: I gave (. . .) my book.

    1. You gave your pen to (. . .).
    2. You wrote a letter to (. . .).
    3. You sent a package to (. . .).
    4. You told a funny story to (. . .).
    5. You showed a photograph to (. . .).
    6. You sent a check to the telephone company.
    7. You passed your dictionary to (. . .).
    8. You handed your notebook to (. . .).
    9. You lent *(an amount of money)* to (. . .).

■ **EXERCISE 47—ORAL:**   Complete the sentences using the words in *italics*.

    1. *a letter, my sister*   I wrote . . . yesterday.
       → *I wrote a letter to my sister yesterday.*
       → *I wrote my sister a letter yesterday.*

    2. *my parents, a telegram*   I sent . . . two days ago.
    3. *some candy, her children*   Mrs. Kelly gave . . . after dinner.
    4. *her car, me*   Sue is going to lend . . . tomorrow.
    5. *the class, a joke*   Sam told . . . yesterday.
    6. *a letter, the newspaper*   I'm going to write . . . .
    7. *the scissors, John*   Did you hand . . . ?
    8. *me, the soy sauce*   Could you please pass . . . ?
    9. *Liz, a picture*   Mr. Schwartz showed . . . of his baby daughter.
    10. *the students, some good advice*   Yesterday the teacher gave . . . .

■ **EXERCISE 48—ORAL (BOOKS CLOSED):** Perform the action. Answer the question.

Example: Give your book to (. . .). What did you do?
Response: I gave my book to (. . .). OR: I gave (. . .) my book.

1. Pass your dictionary to (. . .).
2. Please hand me your pen/pencil.
3. Lend (. . .) some money.
4. Tell (. . .) your name.
5. Please pass my pen to (. . .).
6. Give (. . .) some good advice.
7. Show (. . .) a picture.
8. Write (. . .) a note and pass it to him/her.
9. Give (. . .) a gift.
10. Please hand that piece of chalk to me.

8-17 INDIRECT OBJECTS: USING *FOR*

(a) Bob opened | *the door* | *for Mary.* |
                    direct obj.   INDIRECT obj.
(b) Sue answered | *a question* | *for me.* |
                     direct obj .   INDIRECT obj.
(c) INCORRECT: *Sue answered me a question.*
(d) INCORRECT: *Ken opened Anita the door.*
	With some verbs, *for* is used with the indirect object. With these verbs, the indirect object follows the direct object. *For* is not omitted. The position of the indirect object is not changed.

VERBS FOLLOWED BY INDIRECT OBJECTS WITH *FOR* *answer* He *answered* a question *for me.* *cash* The teller *cashed* a check *for me.* *fix* Can you *fix* my car *for me*? *open* Mr. Smith *opened* the door *for his wife.* *pronounce* I *pronounced* the word *for the students.* *translate* I *translated* a letter *for my brother.*	Notice in the examples: All of the sentences give the idea that someone is helping another person.

CAN YOU FIX IT FOR ME?

■ **EXERCISE 49:** Complete the sentences by adding *for* or *to*.

1. The teacher answered a question _____ me.

2. I opened the door _____ my mother.

3. My roommate translated a newspaper story _____ me.

4. Fred gave some candy _____ his girlfriend.

5. The teller cashed a check _____ me.

6. The mechanic fixed my car _____ me.

7. Mrs. Baker handed the baby _____ her husband.

8. The teacher pronounced "bat" and "but" _____ the students.

9. Our landlord fixed the air conditioner _____ us.

10. Could you please answer a question _____ me?

11. My hands are wet. Could you please open this jar of pickles _____ me?

■ **EXERCISE 50—ORAL (BOOKS CLOSED):** Ask and answer questions.
      STUDENT A: Use *"Could you please . . . for me?"*
      STUDENT B: Answer the question.

Example: open the window
STUDENT A: Could you please open the window for me?
STUDENT B: Certainly. / I'd be happy to. / Sure.

1. answer a question
2. translate a word
3. pronounce a word
4. cash a check
5. fix *(name of something)*
6. open the door

■ **EXERCISE 51—ORAL (BOOKS CLOSED):** Ask and answer questions.

STUDENT A: Ask a question using *"**Could you please . . . ?**"* Use *me, to me,* or *for me* in your question.

STUDENT B: Answer the question.

Example: pass the butter
STUDENT A: Could you please pass me the butter/pass the butter to me?
STUDENT B: Certainly. / I'd be happy to. / Sure.

1. pass the salt
2. hand a napkin
3. pass the salt and pepper
4. answer a question
5. translate this paragraph

6. pronounce this word
7. open the door
8. lend your dictionary
9. give *(name of something in the classroom)*
10. fix *(name of something)*

8-18 INDIRECT OBJECTS WITH *BUY, GET, MAKE*

(a) Tina **bought** a gift **for us**. (b) Tina **bought us** a gift. (c) I **got** a new toy **for my son**. (d) I **got my son** a new toy. (e) Tom **made** lunch **for his wife**. (f) Tom **made his wife** lunch.	With the verbs **buy**, **get**, and **make**, two patterns are possible: • **for** introduces the indirect object, OR • the indirect object precedes the direct object.

■ **EXERCISE 52—ORAL:** Complete the sentences. Use the words in parentheses.

1. I bought . . . *(Jim, a new hat)*
   → *I bought a new hat for Jim.*
   → *I bought Jim a new hat.*

2. Jack got . . . *(a stuffed animal, his daughter)*

3. I bought . . . *(some gloves, Robert)*

4. I made . . . *(Mike, a cake)*

5. Carmen got . . . *(a new television set, her parents)*

6. Eric bought . . . *(a necklace, his mother)*

7. Oscar made . . . *(his guests, dinner)*

8. Heidi bought . . . *(a nice birthday gift, her brother)*

9. Could you please get . . . *(a glass of water, me)*

8-19 INDIRECT OBJECTS WITH *EXPLAIN* AND *INTRODUCE*

(a) The teacher **explained** the grammar **to us**. (b) Anna **introduced** her sister **to me**. (c) INCORRECT: *She explained us the grammar.* (d) INCORRECT: *Anna introduced me her sister.*	With the verbs **explain** and **introduce**: • **to** is used with the indirect object, and • the indirect object always follows the direct object.

■ **EXERCISE 53—ORAL:**   Complete the sentences. Use the words in parentheses.

1. Elizabeth explained . . . *(me, the problem)*
   → *Elizabeth explained the problem to me.*
2. The professor explained . . . *(the students, the chemistry formula)*
3. Tina introduced . . . *(her son, me)*
4. Mr. Schwartz explained . . . *(the doctor, his problem)*
5. Could you please translate . . . *(me, this sentence)*
6. Could you please explain . . . *(me, this sentence)*
7. Fred told . . . *(me, his ideas)*
8. I explained . . . *(my husband, Fred's ideas)*

■ **EXERCISE 54:**   Add the word(s) in parentheses. If necessary, add **to** or **for**.

1. *(Bob)* I wrote a letter.
   → *I wrote Bob a letter.*   OR: *I wrote a letter to Bob.* ✱
2. *(my cousin)* I sent a postcard.

3. *(me)* The teacher answered a question.

4. *(his girlfriend)* Jim opened the car door.

5. *(the bride and groom)* Ann Miller gave a nice wedding present.

6. *(the class)* The teacher pronounced the new vocabulary words.

7. *(us)* The teacher explained the meaning of the word.

8. *(my roommate)* I translated the title of a book.

9. *(me)* My friend answered the phone because my hands were full.

10. *(the University of Texas)* I sent an application.

✱*I wrote a letter for Bob* is possible, but it has a special meaning: It gives the idea that I helped Bob. (For example: Bob broke his hand. He can't write. He wanted to write a letter. I helped him by writing the letter.)

11. *(his wife)* Ron fixed the sewing machine.

12. *(us)* Don told a funny joke at the party.

13. *(me)* Jane explained her problems.

14. *(me)* My father wrote a letter.

15. *(the teacher)* Samir showed a picture of his family.

16. *(my friend)* I bought a gift.

■ **EXERCISE 55—ORAL (BOOKS CLOSED):** Answer the questions in complete sentences.

Example: It's (. . .)'s birthday next week. What are you going to give her/him?
[Followup: What is (Student A) going to do?]
STUDENT A: A box of candy.
TEACHER: What is (Student A) going to do?
STUDENT B: She/He's going to give (. . .) a box of candy for her/his birthday. OR
She/He's going to give a box of candy to (. . .) for her/his birthday.

1. (. . .) is getting married next month. What are you going to give her/him?
[Followup: What is (Student A) going to do?]

2. Take something out of your pocket or purse and hand it to (. . .).
[What did (Student A) do?]

3. Please explain the location of your country to (. . .).
[What did (Student A) explain?]

4. (. . .), ask (. . .) a question. (. . .), answer the question for her/him.
[What did (Student A) do and (Student B) do?]

5. (. . .) needs some money desperately to pay her/his rent so s/he won't get kicked out
of her/his apartment. How much money will you lend her/him?
[What is (Student A) going to do?]

6. Hide a small item in your hand. Show it to (. . .), but don't show it to (. . .).
[What did (Student A) do?]

7. Say a word in your native language and then translate it into English for (. . .).
[What did (Student A) do?]

8. Teach (. . .) how to say a word in your native language. Pronounce it for (. . .)
several times.   [What did (Student A) do?]

9. Get a piece of chalk for (. . .). [What did (Student A) do?]

10. Make a paper airplane for (. . .). [What did (Student A) do?]

■ **EXERCISE 56—WRITTEN:** Write complete sentences by adding DIRECT OBJECTS and INDIRECT OBJECTS.

1. I wrote _____ _____ yesterday.

2. I sent _____ _____ last week.

3. Please pass _____ _____.

4. The taxi driver opened _____ _____.

5. (. . .) gave _____ _____.

6. Could you please pronounce _____ _____?

7. Could you please lend _____ _____?

8. (. . .) translated _____ _____.

9. Could you please answer _____ _____?

10. My friend explained _____ _____.

11. I bought _____ _____.

12. Could you please get _____ _____?

■ **EXERCISE 57—REVIEW:** Choose the correct completion.

1. This newspaper is yours. That newspaper is _____.
    A. our   B. ours   C. our's   D. ours'

2. The teacher gave a test paper to every _____ in the class.
    A. student   B. students   C. of student   D. of students

3. Rosa is a _____ woman.
    A. beautiful Mexican young   C. Mexican beautiful young
    B. beautiful young Mexican   D. young beautiful Mexican

4. _____ the students in our class have dark hair.
    A. All most of   C. Almost
    B. Almost of   D. Almost all of

5. I handed _____.
    A. to the teacher my book   C. my book the teacher
    B. my book to the teacher   D. my book for the teacher

6. I had some _____ soup for lunch.
    A. vegetable good   C. vegetables good
    B. good vegetables   D. good vegetable

7. Jack introduced me to one _____.
   A. friends   B. of his friend   C. of his friends   D. his friends

8. My _____ name is Ernesto.
   A. father   B. fathers   C. fathers'   D. father's

9. Ahmed pronounced _____.
   A. for me his name   C. his name to me
   B. me his name   D. his name for me

10. _____ books are these?
    A. Who's   B. Whose   C. Who   D. Who are

■ **EXERCISE 58—ERROR ANALYSIS:** Find and correct the mistakes.

1. I bought an airplane's ticket. Was expensive.

2. Some of those book's is mine.

3. Hiroki is a japanese businessman.

4. Theres an old big tree in our backyard.

5. Did you give to Jim my message?

6. The cat licked it's paw.

7. Everybody want to be happy.

8. One of the building on Main Street is the post office.

9. Whose that woman?

10. What are those peoples names?

11. Is the bedroom's window open?

12. Mr. and Mrs. Swan like their's apartment. Its large and comfortable.

13. I walk in the park every days.

14. Who's book is this?

15. I'am studying English.

16. Tina her last name Miller.

17. Please explain me this sentence.

18. My roommate desks are always messy.

19. Could you pronounce me this word?

20. I know the name's of almost of the students' in my class.

■ **EXERCISE 59—REVIEW:** Play this game in small groups. Think of a NOUN. Describe this noun to your group by giving clues. Don't mention the noun. The group will guess the noun you're thinking of.

Examples:
STUDENT A: I'm thinking of a kind of plant. It's small and colorful. It smells good.
GROUP: A flower!

STUDENT B: I'm thinking of a person. She has short black hair. She's wearing a blue sweater and a black skirt today.
GROUP: That's too easy! Yoko!

STUDENT C: I'm thinking of a very big cat. It's a wild animal.
GROUP: A lion!
STUDENT C: No. It's orange and black. It lives in Asia. It has stripes.
GROUP: A tiger!

■ **EXERCISE 60—REVIEW:** Bring to class an object from your country. In a small group, describe your object and tell your classmates about it: What is it? How is it used? Why is it special? Answer questions from the group.

When all of the groups finish discussing the objects, all of the objects should be brought to the center of the room.

STUDENT A: Choose one of the objects. Ask questions about it. Find out who it belongs to and what it is. (The owner of the object should NOT speak. People from the owner's group will give Student A the necessary information.)
STUDENT B: Choose another one of the objects and ask questions.
STUDENT C: Etc.

After all of the objects have been discussed, choose five of them to write about. Write a short paragraph on each object. What is it? What does it look like? Whose is it? What's it for? Why is it special? Why is it interesting to you? Etc.

8-20 MORE IRREGULAR VERBS

become – became	feed – fed
bend – bent	fight – fought
bite – bit	hide – hid
build – built	hold – held
shake – shook	

■ **EXERCISE 61—ORAL (BOOKS CLOSED):** Practice using the IRREGULAR VERBS in the above list.

1. *become - became* When strangers meet, they can become friends. I met (. . .) *(a length of time)* ago. We became friends. What happened between (. . .) and me?

2. *bend - bent* When I drop something, I bend over to pick it up. I just dropped my pen, and then I bent over to pick it up. What did I do?

3. *bite - bit* Sometimes dogs bite people. Yesterday my friend's dog bit my hand while we were playing. What happened to my hand?

4. *build - built* I have some friends who know how to build houses. They built their own house next to the river. What did my friends do?

5. *feed - fed* I have a *(dog, cat, parrot, etc.)*. I have to feed it every day. Yesterday I fed it once in the morning and once in the evening. What did I do yesterday?

6. *fight - fought* People fight in wars. People fight diseases. They fight for freedom and equality. My country fought a war *(against another country in a time period)*. What happened *(in that time period)*?

7. *hide - hid* I have a coin in my hand. Close your eyes while I hide it. Okay, open your eyes. I hid the coin. Where's the coin? Why don't you know?

8. *hold - held* When it rains, I hold my umbrella. Yesterday it rained. I held my umbrella. What did I do yesterday?

9. *shake - shook* People sometimes shake their finger or their head. Sometimes they shake when they're cold. Right now I'm shaking my finger/my head. What did I just do?

■ **EXERCISE 62:** Complete the sentences. Use the words in parentheses.

1. I *(hide)* _____ my husband's birthday present in the closet yesterday.

2. A: Ow!
   B: What's the matter?

   A: I *(bite)* _____ my tongue.

3. When I asked Dennis a question, he *(shake)* _____ his head no.

4. A: I've lost touch with some of our childhood friends. What happened to Greg Jones?

   B: He *(become)* _____ a doctor.
   A: What happened to Sandy Peterson?

   B: She *(become)* _____ a lawyer.

5. I offered the child a red lollipop or a green lollipop. He *(choose)* _____ the red one.

6. Doug is a new father. He felt very happy when he *(hold)* _____ his baby for the first time.

7. Nancy and Tom saved money. They didn't buy a bookcase for their new apartment.

   They *(build)* _____ one.

8. We saw a strong man at the circus. He *(bend)* _____ an iron bar.

9. A: Why did the children fight?

   B: They *(fight)* _____ because both of them wanted the same toy.

10. Diane is a computer programmer.

   Yesterday she *(feed)* _____ information into the computer.

■ **EXERCISE 63:** Complete the sentences with the correct form of the verbs from the given list.

become	*build*	*hide*
bend	*feed*	*hold*
bite	*fight*	✔ *shake*

1. When my dog got out of the lake, it _____*shook*_____ itself. Dogs always

   _____*shake*_____ themselves when they're wet.

2. Many countries in the world _____ in World War II.

3. Sometimes snakes _____ people. My cousin Jake died after a

   poisonous snake _____ him.

4. My daughter _____ a table in her woodworking class in high school.

5. When Kathy dropped her pen, Sam _____ over and picked it up for her.

6. The baby is sleeping peacefully. She's not hungry. Her mother _____ her before she put her in bed.

7. Mike stole a spoon from the restaurant. He _____ it in his pocket before he walked out of the restaurant.

8. David is a Canadian citizen. Maria was born in Puerto Rico, but when she married David, she _____ a Canadian citizen too.

■ **EXERCISE 64—ORAL (BOOKS CLOSED):** In order to practice IRREGULAR VERBS, answer *yes*.

Example: Did you write a letter yesterday?
Response: Yes, I did. I wrote a letter yesterday.

1. Did you fly to *(this city)*?
2. Did you drink a cup of tea this morning?
3. Did you come to class yesterday?
4. Did you go downtown yesterday?
5. Did you eat breakfast this morning?
6. Did you lend some money to (. . .)?
7. Did you lose your pen yesterday? Did you find it?
8. Did you give your dictionary to (. . .)?
9. Did you throw your book to (. . .)? (. . .), did you catch it?
10. Did someone steal your wallet? Did you get it back?
11. Did you wake up at seven this morning?
12. Did you get up at seven this morning?
13. Did the wind blow yesterday?
14. Did you shut the door?
15. Did class begin at (. . .)?
16. Did you say hello to (. . .)?
17. Did you tell (. . .) to sit down? (. . .), did you sit down?
18. Did you hear my last question?
19. Did you teach your daughter/son to count to ten?
20. Did you bring your books to class today?
21. Did you forget your books?
22. Did you see (. . .) yesterday?
23. Did you meet (. . .)'s wife?
24. Did you leave your sunglasses at the restaurant?
25. Did you read the newspaper this morning?
26. Did you go shopping yesterday?
27. Did you drive your car to school today?
28. Did you ride a horse to school today?

29. Did a barber cut your hair?
30. Did you run to class this morning?
31. Did your pen cost *(an amount of money)*?
32. Did you understand my question?
33. Did you come to class yesterday?
34. Did you make a mistake?
35. Did you take the bus to school today?
36. Did you write a letter yesterday? Did you send it?
37. Did the telephone ring?
38. Did you break your arm?
39. Did you shake your head?
40. Did you draw a picture?
41. Did you bend your elbow?
42. Did you win a million dollars?
43. Did you feel good yesterday?
44. Did you feed the birds at the park?
45. Did you bite your finger?
46. Did you hurt your finger?
47. Did you hold (. . .)'s hand?
48. Did you build a bookcase?
49. Did you stand at the bus stop?
50. Did you sing in the shower this morning?
51. Did you grow up in *(country)*?
52. Did you become an adult?
53. Did *(name of a sports team)* win yesterday?
54. Did you fall down yesterday?
55. Did you think about me yesterday?
56. Did you fight yesterday?
57. Which pen do you want? Did you choose this one?
58. Did you hide your money under your mattress?
59. Did your car hit a telephone pole yesterday?
60. Did you put your books under your desk?

CHAPTER 9
Making Comparisons

9-1 COMPARISONS: USING *THE SAME (AS)*, *SIMILAR (TO)*, AND *DIFFERENT (FROM)*

THE SAME (AS)	SIMILAR (TO)	DIFFERENT (FROM)
A and B are **the same**. A is **the same as** B.	C and D are **similar**. C is **similar to** D.	E and F are **different**. E is **different from** F.

■ **EXERCISE 1—ORAL:** Which of the pictures are the same, similar, or different?

 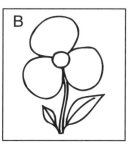 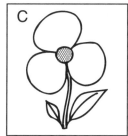 

1. Are Pictures A and B the same?

2. Are Pictures A and C the same?

3. Are Pictures A and C similar?

4. Are Pictures A and C different?

5. Are Pictures C and D similar?

6. Are Pictures C and D different?

■ **EXERCISE 2:** Complete the sentences. Use *the same (as)*, *similar (to)*, and *different (from)* in your completions.

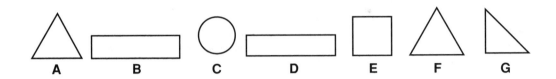

1. A _____*is the same as*_____ F.

2. D and E _____*are similar* OR: *are different**_____.

3. C _____ D.

4. B _____ D.

5. B and D _____.

6. C and D _____.

7. A and F _____.

8. F and G _____.

9. F _____ G.

10. G _____ A and F, but

_____ C.

■ **EXERCISE 3—ERROR ANALYSIS:** Find and correct the mistakes.

1. A rectangle is similar a square.

2. Pablo and Rita come from same country.

3. Girls and boys are differents. Girls are different to boys.

4. My cousin is the same age with my brother.

5. Dogs are similar with wolves.

6. Jim and I started to speak at same time.

_____

*Similar gives the idea that two things are the same in some ways (e.g., both D and E have four edges) but different in other ways (e.g., D is a rectangle and E is a square).

■ **EXERCISE 4:** Answer the questions.

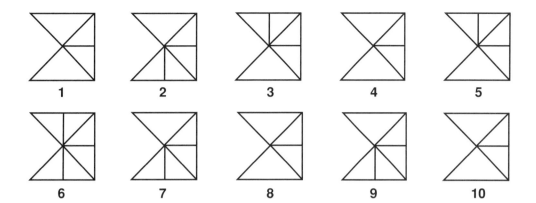

1 2 3 4 5

6 7 8 9 10

1. Which of the figures are the same?

2. Is there at least one figure that is different from all the rest?

3. How many triangles are there in figure 1? *(answer: Seven.)*

4. How many triangles are there in figure 2?

5. How many triangles are there in figure 6?

■ **EXERCISE 5—ORAL (BOOKS CLOSED):** Practice using *the same (as)*, *similar (to)*, and *different (from)*.

Example: Look at (. . .)'s clothes and (. . .)'s clothes. What is different about the clothes they are wearing today?

Response: Their shoes are different. Mr. Lopez is wearing running shoes, and Mr. Gow is wearing sandals.

1. Look around the room. Name things that are the same.
2. Look around the room. Name things that are similar but not the same.
3. Find two pens that are the same length. Find two pieces of paper that are the same size. Find two notebooks that are different sizes.
4. Find two people in the class who are wearing (earrings). Are their (earrings) the same, similar, or different?
5. Who in the class has a (notebook, briefcase, bookbag) that is similar to yours? Does anyone have a (notebook, briefcase, bookbag) that is the same as yours?
6. Do any of the people in this room have the same hairstyle? Name two people who have similar hairstyles.
7. Whose shirt is the same color as yours today? Name some things in this room that are the same color. Name things that are similar colors.
8. Do any of the people in this room come from the same country? Who? Name two people who come from different countries.
9. Name an animal that is similar to a tiger. Name a bird that is similar to a duck.
10. Are Egypt and Italy on the same continent? Egypt and Algeria? Thailand and Korea? Mexico and Brazil?

9-2 COMPARISONS: USING *LIKE* AND *ALIKE*

You have a ballpoint pen with blue ink. I have a ballpoint pen with blue ink. (a) Your pen *is like* my pen. (b) Your pen and my pen *are alike*. (c) Our pens *are alike*.	*like* = similar to *alike* = similar *Like* and *alike* have the same meaning, but the sentence patterns are different: This + *be* + *like* + that. This and that + *be* + *alike*.

■ **EXERCISE 6:** Complete the sentences with *like* and *alike*.

1. You and I have similar books. In other words, your book is ____like____ mine. Our books are ____alike____.

2. Mr. Chang and I have similar coats. In other words, Mr. Chang's coat is _____ mine. Our coats are _____.

3. Ken and Sue have similar cars. In other words, their cars are _____.

4. You and I have similar hats. In other words, your hat is _____ mine.

5. A town is _____ a city in some ways.

6. A foot and a hand are _____ in some ways, but different in other ways.

7. A dormitory and an apartment building are _____ in many ways.

8. A motorcyle is _____ a bicycle in some ways.

■ **EXERCISE 7—ORAL:** Make sentences with *like*. Compare the things in Column A with the things in Column B. Discuss how the two things you are comparing are similar.

Example: A pencil is like a pen in some ways. They are both writing instruments.

COLUMN A	COLUMN B
an alley	a glass
a bus	a human hand
a bush	a lemon
a cup	a chair
a hill	a mountain
honey	an ocean
a monkey's hand	✔ a pen
an orange	a street
✔ a pencil	sugar
a sea	a suit coat
a sofa	a taxi
a sports jacket	a tree

9-3 THE COMPARATIVE: USING -ER AND MORE

Mary is 25 years old. John is 20 years old. (a) Mary is **older than** John. (b) Health is **more important than** money. (c) INCORRECT: *Mary is more old than John.* (d) INCORRECT: *Health is importanter than money.*	When we use adjectives (e.g., *old, important*) to compare two people or two things, the adjectives have special forms: In (a): we add **-er** to an adjective, OR In (b): we use **more** in front of an adjective. The use of **-er** or **more** is called the COMPARATIVE FORM.
	Notice in the examples: **than** follows the comparative form: *older **than**, more important **than**.*

	ADJECTIVE / COMPARATIVE	
ADJECTIVES WITH ONE SYLLABLE	**old** **older** **cheap** **cheaper** **big** **bigger**	Add **-er** to one-syllable adjectives. Spelling note: if an adjective ends in one vowel and one consonant, double the consonant: *big–bigger, fat–fatter, thin–thinner, hot–hotter.*
ADJECTIVES THAT END IN -Y	**pretty** **prettier** **funny** **funnier**	If an adjective ends in **-y**, change the **-y** to **i** and add **-er**.
ADJECTIVES WITH TWO OR MORE SYLLABLES	**famous** **more famous** **important** **more important** **interesting** **more interesting**	Use **more** in front of adjectives that have two or more syllables (except adjectives that end in **-y**).
IRREGULAR COMPARATIVE FORMS	**good** **better** **bad** **worse** **far** **farther/further**	The comparative forms of **good, bad**, and **far** are irregular.

■ **EXERCISE 8:** Write the comparative forms for the following ADJECTIVES.

1. old   *older than*

2. small _____

3. big _____

4. important _____

5. easy _____

6. difficult _____

7. long _____

8. heavy _____

9. sweet _____

10. expensive _____

11. hot _____

12. cheap _____

13. good _____

14. bad _____

15. far _____

16. lazy _____

■ **EXERCISE 9:** Complete the sentences. Use the COMPARATIVE form of the words in *italics*.

1. *comfortable*   This chair is _____*more comfortable than*_____ that chair.

2. *large*   Your apartment is _____ mine.

3. *warm*   It's _____ today _____ yesterday.

4. *dark*   Tom's mustache is _____ Don's.

5. *important*   Love is _____ money.

6. *lazy*   I'm _____ my roommate.

7. *tall*   My brother is _____ I am.★

8. *heavy*   Iron is _____ wood.

9. *difficult*   My physics course is _____ my math course.

10. *good*   Nadia's English is _____ her husband's.

11. *long*   The Nile River is _____ the Mississippi.

12. *intelligent*   A dog is _____ a chicken.

13. *good*   My wife's cooking is _____ mine.

14. *bad*   My cooking is _____ my wife's.

15. *short*   My little finger is _____ my middle finger.

16. *pretty*   This dress is _____ that one.

17. *far*   Your apartment is _____ from school _____ mine.

18. *strong*   A horse is _____ a person.

19. *curly*   Ken's hair is _____ mine.

20. *beautiful*   A rose is _____ a weed.

_____

★Formal written English: *My brother is taller than I (am).*
Informal spoken English: *My brother is taller than me.*

■ **EXERCISE 10:** Complete the sentences. Use the COMPARATIVE form of the words in *italics*.

1. *good*   The weather today is _____ it was yesterday.

2. *bad*   The weather yesterday was _____ it is today.

3. *funny*   This story is _____ that story.

4. *interesting* This book is _____ that book.

5. *smart*   Joe is _____ his brother.

6. *famous*   A movie star is _____ I am.

7. *wide*   A highway is _____ an alley.

8. *deep*   The Pacific Ocean is _____ the Mediterranean Sea.

9. *confusing*   This story is _____ that story.

10. *hot*   Thailand is _____ Korea.

11. *thin*   A giraffe's neck is _____ an elephant's neck.

12. *far*   My house is _____ from downtown

                 _____ your house is.

13. *good*   Reading a good book is _____ watching television.

14. *easy*   My English class is _____ my history class.

15. *nervous*   The groom was _____

                 at the wedding _____ the bride.

■ **EXERCISE 11—ORAL:**   Compare the following. Use the ADJECTIVE in parentheses. Use *more* or *-er*.

Example: A mouse is smaller than an elephant.

1. a mouse
   an elephant
   (small)

2. my old shoes
   my new shoes
   (comfortable)

3. your hair
   my hair
   (dark)

4. my arm
   your arm
   (long)

5. biology
   chemistry
   (interesting)

6. I
   my brother
   (thin)

7. my hair
   her hair
   (curly)

8. her hair
   his hair
   (straight)

9. this book
   that one
   (good)

10. the weather here
    the weather in my hometown
    (bad)

11. this chapter
    Chapter 8
    (easy)

12. Japanese grammar
    English grammar
    (difficult)

■ **EXERCISE 12—ORAL (BOOKS CLOSED):**   Practice comparative forms.

A. Put several different books in a central place. Compare one to another, using the given adjectives.

Example: big
Response: This book is bigger than that book/that one.

1. large
2. interesting
3. small
4. heavy

5. difficult
6. easy
7. good
8. bad

9. expensive
10. cheap
11. thick
12. important

B. The following adjectives describe a man named Bob. A man named Jack does not have the same qualities. Draw pictures of Bob and Jack on the board. Compare Bob to Jack.

Example: tall
Response: Bob is taller than Jack.

1. tall
2. strong
3. lazy
4. intelligent

5. young
6. happy
7. kind
8. generous

9. friendly★
10. responsible
11. famous
12. busy

★The comparative of *friendly* has two possible forms: *friendlier than* or *more friendly than*.

■ **EXERCISE 13:** Complete the sentences. Use the COMPARATIVE form of the words in the list (or your own words).

big	*easy*	*important*
bright	*expensive*	*intelligent*
cheap	*fast*	*large*
cold	*high*	*small*
comfortable	*hot*	*sweet*

1. An elephant is _____*bigger than / larger than*_____ a mouse.

2. A lemon is sour. An orange is _____ a lemon.

3. The weather today is _____ it was yesterday.

4. A diamond costs a lot of money. A diamond is _____ a ruby.

5. I can afford a radio, but not a TV set. A radio is _____ a TV set.

6. An airplane moves quickly. An airplane is _____ an automobile.

7. A lake is _____ an ocean.

8. A person can think logically. A person is _____ an animal.

9. Hills are low. Mountains are _____ hills.

10. The sun gives off a lot of light. The sun is _____ the moon.

11. Texas is a large state, but Alaska is

_____ Texas.

12. Sometimes my feet hurt when I wear high heels. Bedroom slippers are

_____

shoes with high heels.

13. Arithmetic isn't difficult. Arithmetic is

_____ algebra.

14. Good health is _____ money.

■ **EXERCISE 14—ORAL (BOOKS CLOSED):**   Compare the following.

Example: an elephant to a mouse
Response: An elephant is bigger than a mouse / more intelligent than a mouse, etc.

1. an orange to a lemon
2. a lake to an ocean
3. good health to money
4. a radio to a TV set
5. an airplane to an automobile
6. (Alaska) to (Texas)
7. a person to an animal
8. the sun to the moon
9. a mountain to a hill
10. arithmetic to algebra
11. a diamond to a ruby
12. bedroom slippers to high heels
13. a child to an adult
14. a horse to a person
15. the Nile River to the Mississippi River
16. your little finger to your ring finger
17. love to money
18. your hair to (. . .)'s hair
19. food in *(your country)* to food in *(another country)*
20. the weather today to the weather yesterday

■ **EXERCISE 15—ORAL (BOOKS CLOSED):**   Make sentences by using **-er/more** with these ADJECTIVES.

Example: large
Response: Canada is larger than Mexico. / My feet are larger than yours. / etc.

1. tall
2. important
3. cold
4. curly
5. expensive
6. long
7. easy
8. comfortable
9. old
10. strong
11. small
12. intelligent
13. big
14. heavy
15. cheap
16. sweet
17. high
18. interesting
19. good
20. bad

■ **EXERCISE 16:**   Write a sentence by using **-er/more** with an ADJECTIVE in the list in Exercise 15 above. Tear the sentence into pieces, with one word or phrase on each piece. Give the pieces to a classmate who will reassemble your sentence. Repeat this exercise several times, using a different adjective for each new sentence you write.

John is 21 years old. Mary is 21 years old. (a) John *is as old as* Mary.	Notice the pattern: **as** + *adjective* + **as**
	In (a): Their ages are the same.
(b) This watch *is as expensive as* that watch.	In (b): The price of the watches is the same.
Fred is 20 years old. Jean is 21 years old. (c) Fred *isn't as old as* Jean. (d) Fred *is younger than* Jean.	(c) and (d) have the same meaning.
(e) This book *isn't as expensive as* that book. (f) This book *is cheaper than* that book.	(e) and (f) have the same meaning.
(g) This book *isn't as expensive as* that book. (h) This book *is less expensive than* that book.	(g) and (h) have the same meaning. **Less** is the opposite of **more**. **Less** is used with adjectives that have two or more syllables (except most adjectives that end in **-y**). **Less** is usually not used with one-syllable adjectives or adjectives that end in **-y**. INCORRECT: *Fred is less old than Jean.* CORRECT: *Fred isn't as old as Jean.* *Fred is younger than Jean.*

■ **EXERCISE 17:**   Complete the following sentences by using **as . . . as** and the ADJECTIVE in *italics*.

1. *tall*   Mary is _____*as tall as*_____ her brother.

2. *sweet*   A lemon isn't _____ an orange.

3. *big*   A donkey isn't _____ a horse.

4. *friendly*   People in this city are _____ the people
                 in my hometown.

5. *dark*   Paul's hair isn't _____ his brother's.

6. *cold*   The weather isn't _____ today

                 _____ yesterday.

7. *pretty*   This dress is _____ that one.

8. *expensive*   A pencil isn't _____ a pen.

■ **EXERCISE 18:** Make sentences with the same meaning by using **less**, if possible.

1. This book isn't as expensive as that book.
   → *This book is less expensive than that book.*

2. Bob isn't as old as Jim. → *(no change)*

3. Arithmetic isn't as difficult as algebra.

4. Arithmetic isn't as hard as algebra.

5. This chair isn't as comfortable as that chair.

6. This box isn't as heavy as that box.

7. A hill isn't as high as a mountain.

8. Swimming isn't as dangerous as boxing.

9. I'm not as tall as my brother.

10. This letter isn't as important as that letter.

■ **EXERCISE 19:** Make sentences with the same meaning by using **as . . . as** with the ADJECTIVE in parentheses.

1. Bob is younger than Sally. *(old)*
   → *Bob isn't as old as Sally.*

2. This book is less expensive than that one. *(expensive)*
   → *This book isn't as expensive as that one.*

3. I'm shorter than my sister. *(tall)*

4. This exercise is more difficult than the last one. *(easy)*

5. My new shoes are less comfortable than my old shoes. *(comfortable)*

6. My little finger is shorter than my index finger. *(long)*

7. A radio is less expensive than a TV set. *(expensive)*

8. This book is worse than that book. *(good)*

9. My apartment is smaller than yours. *(big)*

10. In my opinion, chemistry is less interesting than psychology. *(interesting)*

■ **EXERCISE 20:** Make sentences with the same meaning by using *as . . . as*.

1. This room is smaller than that room.
    → *This room isn't as big as that room.*

2. An animal is less intelligent than a human being.

3. Soda pop is less expensive than fruit juice.

4. The Mississippi River is shorter than the Nile River.

5. Tom's pronunciation is worse than Sue's.

6. Algebra is more difficult than arithmetic.

7. Money is less important than good health.

8. American coffee is weaker than Turkish coffee.

9. A wooden chair is less comfortable than a sofa.

10. A van is smaller than a bus.

■ **EXERCISE 21—ORAL (BOOKS CLOSED):**   Work in pairs. Practice making comparisons.

> STUDENT A: Your book is open.
> STUDENT B: Your book is closed. Respond in complete sentences.

Example: Name something that is sweeter than an apple.
STUDENT A: What's sweeter than an apple? / Can you name something that is sweeter than an apple? / Name something that is sweeter than an apple.
STUDENT B: Candy is sweeter than an apple.

1. Name a country that is larger than Mexico.
2. Name a planet that is closer to or farther away from the sun than the earth.
3. Name someone in the class who isn't as old as (I am, you are).
4. Name an animal that is more dangerous than a zebra.
5. Name an animal that is as dangerous as a wild tiger.
6. Name a bird that is larger than a chicken.
7. Name something that is more expensive than a diamond ring.
8. Name something that is less expensive than *(an object in this room)*.
9. Name someone who is more famous than *(name of a famous person)*.

Switch roles.
10. Name something that is more interesting than *(name of a field of study)*.
11. Name something that is less important than good health.
12. Name a place that is as far away from here as *(name of a place)*.
13. Name an ocean that is smaller than the Pacific Ocean.
14. Name an animal that is stronger than a horse.
15. Name an animal that isn't as strong as a horse.
16. Name a game that is, in your opinion, more exciting than *(name of a sport)*.
17. Name a sport that is less popular internationally than *(name of a sport)*.
18. Name a place that is more beautiful than this city.

■ **EXERCISE 22:**   Complete the following with your own words.

1. I'm taller _____

2. I'm not as old _____

3. A monkey isn't as big _____

4. American food isn't as good _____

5. An ocean is deeper and wider _____

6. An apple is less expensive _____

7. It's warmer / colder today _____

8. _____'s hair isn't as curly _____

9. A hill isn't as high _____

10. A dog is less intelligent _____ but more intelligent

_____

11. _____'s hair is darker _____

12. A hotel room is less comfortable _____

13. Moonlight isn't as bright _____

14. Money is less important _____

15. English grammar isn't as difficult _____

16. Earth is closer to the sun _____

17. Venezuela isn't as far south _____

18. Tokyo isn't as far north _____

19. People in _____ are friendlier _____

20. Children are less powerful _____

9-5 USING *BUT*

(a)	John is rich, ***but*** Mary is poor.	***But*** gives the idea that "This is the opposite of that."
(b)	The weather was cold, ***but*** we were warm inside our house.	A comma usually precedes ***but***.

■ **EXERCISE 23:** Complete the following sentences by using ADJECTIVES.

1. An orange is sweet, but a lemon is _____*sour.*_____

2. The weather is hot today, but it was _____ yesterday.

3. These dishes are clean, but those dishes are _____

4. This suitcase is heavy, but that suitcase is _____

5. My hair is light, but my brother's hair is _____

6. These shoes are uncomfortable, but those shoes are _____

7. Linda is tall, but her sister is _____

8. This street is narrow, but that street is _____

9. This exercise is easy, but that exercise is _____

10. My old apartment is big, but my new apartment is _____

11. This food is good, but that food is _____

12. A chicken is stupid, but a human being is _____

13. Smoke is visible, but clean air is _____

14. This answer is right, but that answer is _____

15. This towel is dry, but that towel is _____

16. This cup is full, but that cup is _____

17. This street is noisy, but that street is _____

18. This picture is ugly, but that picture is _____

19. This sentence is confusing, but that sentence is _____

20. This car is safe, but that car is _____

21. A kitten is weak, but a horse is _____

22. This watch is expensive, but that watch is _____

23. Tom is hard-working, but his brother is _____

24. My apartment is messy, but Bob's apartment is always _____

25. A pillow is soft, but a rock is _____

9-6 USING VERBS AFTER *BUT*

	AFFIRMATIVE VERB	+	*but*	+	NEGATIVE VERB	Often the verb phrase following *but* is shortened, as in the examples.
(a)	John *is* rich,		*but*		Mary *isn't*.	
(b)	Balls *are* round,		*but*		boxes *aren't*.	
(c)	I *was* in class,		*but*		Po *wasn't*.	
(d)	Sue *studies* hard,		*but*		Sam *doesn't*.	
(e)	We *like* movies,		*but*		they *don't*.	
(f)	Alex *came*,		*but*		Maria *didn't*.	
(g)	People *can* talk,		*but*		animals *can't*.	
(h)	Olga *will* be there,		*but*		Ivan *won't*.	
	NEGATIVE VERB	+	*but*	+	AFFIRMATIVE VERB	
(i)	Mary *isn't* rich,		*but*		John *is*.	
(j)	Boxes *aren't* round,		*but*		balls *are*.	
(k)	Po *wasn't* in class,		*but*		I *was*.	
(l)	Sam *doesn't* study,		*but*		Sue *does*.	
(m)	They *don't like* cats,		*but*		we *do*.	
(n)	Maria *didn't come*,		*but*		Alex *did*.	
(o)	Animals *can't* talk,		*but*		people *can*.	
(p)	Ivan *won't* be there,		*but*		Olga *will*.	

■ **EXERCISE 24:** Complete each sentence with an appropriate VERB, affirmative or negative.

1. Sara is at home, but her husband _____*isn't*_____.

2. Hiroki isn't at home, but his wife _____.

3. Beds are comfortable, but park benches _____.

4. I wasn't at home last night, but my roommate _____.

5. Kim was in class yesterday, but Anna and Linda _____.

6. Jack wants to go to the zoo, but Barbara _____.

7. I don't want to go to the movie, but my friends _____.

8. Pablo went to the party, but Steve _____.

9. Ahmed can speak French, but I _____.

10. Amanda will be at the meeting, but Helen _____.

11. I was at home yesterday, but my roommate _____.

12. This shirt is clean, but that one _____.

13. These shoes aren't comfortable, but those shoes _____.

14. I like strong coffee, but Karen _____.

15. Mike doesn't write clearly, but Ted _____.

16. I ate breakfast this morning, but my roommate _____.

17. Carol has a car, but Jerry _____.

18. Jerry doesn't have a car, but Carol _____.

19. Ron was at the party, but his wife _____.

20. Ron went to the party, but his wife _____.

21. Ellen can speak Spanish, but her husband _____.

22. Boris can't speak Spanish, but his wife _____.

23. I won't be at home tonight, but Sue _____.

24. Ken will be in class tomorrow, but Chris _____.

25. Amy won't be here tomorrow, but Alice _____.

■ **EXERCISE 25—ORAL (BOOKS CLOSED):** Practice using *but* . . . .

Example: Who in the class was at home last night? Who wasn't at home last night?
TEACHER: Who was at home last night?
STUDENT A: I was.
TEACHER: Who wasn't at home last night?
STUDENT B: I wasn't at home last night.
TEACHER: Summarize, using *but*.
STUDENT C: (Ali) was at home last night, but (Kim) wasn't.

1. Who wears glasses? Who doesn't wear glasses?
2. Who is married? Who isn't married?
3. Who didn't watch TV last night? Who watched TV last night?
4. Who will be in class tomorrow? Who won't be in class tomorrow?
5. Who has a car? Who doesn't have a car?
6. Who studied last night? Who didn't study last night?
7. Who can play *(a musical instrument)*? Who can't play *(that musical instrument)*?
8. Who is hungry right now? Who isn't hungry right now?
9. Who lives in an apartment? Who lives in a house or in a dorm?
10. Who doesn't drink coffee? Who drinks coffee?
11. Who won't be at home tonight? Who will be at home tonight?
12. Who was in class yesterday? Who wasn't in class yesterday?
13. Who can't speak *(a language)*? Who can speak *(a language)*?
14. Who didn't stay home last night? Who stayed home last night?
15. Who has *(a mustache)*? Who doesn't have *(a mustache)*?

■ **EXERCISE 26:** Picture A and Picture B are not the same. There are many differences between A and B. Can you find all of the differences?

Example: There's a wooden chair in Picture A, but there isn't a chair in B.

A

B

■ **EXERCISE 27—ERROR ANALYSIS:** Find and correct the mistakes.

1. My cousin is the same tall as my brother.

2. A blue whale is more large from an elephant.

3. A dog is less small as a wolf.

4. Your handwriting is more better than mine.

5. Robert and Maria aren't same age. Robert is more young than Maria.

6. A lake isn't as deep than an ocean.

■ **EXERCISE 28—WRITTEN:** Write about one or more of the following topics.

1. Write about this city. Compare it to your hometown.
2. Write about your present residence. Compare it to a past residence. For example, compare your new apartment to your old apartment.
3. Write about two members of your family. Compare them.
4. Write about two animals. Compare them.
5. Write about two countries. Compare them.

CHECKLIST OF WORDS USED IN COMPARISONS		
the same (as)	*like*	*-er/more*
similar (to)	*alike*	*less*
different (from)		*as . . . as*
		but

9-7 THE SUPERLATIVE: USING -EST AND MOST

(a) COMPARATIVE: My thumb is **shorter than** my index finger.	The comparative **(-er/more)** compares two things or people.
(b) SUPERLATIVE: My hand has five fingers. My thumb is **the shortest** (finger) of all.	The superlative **(-er/most)** compares three or more things or people.

	ADJECTIVE	COMPARATIVE	SUPERLATIVE
ADJECTIVES WITH ONE SYLLABLE	**old** **big**	**older** (than) **bigger** (than)	**the oldest** (of all) **the biggest** (of all)
ADJECTIVES THAT END IN -Y	**pretty** **easy**	**prettier** (than) **easier** (than)	**the prettiest** (of all) **the easiest** (of all)
ADJECTIVES WITH TWO OR MORE SYLLABLES	**expensive** **important**	**more expensive** (than) **more important** (than)	**the most expensive** (of all) **the most important** (of all)
IRREGULAR FORMS	**good** **bad** **far**	**better** (than) **worse** (than) **farther/further** (than)	**the best** (of all) **the worst** (of all) **the farthest/furthest** (of all)

■ **EXERCISE 29:** Write the comparative and superlative forms of the following ADJECTIVES.

	COMPARATIVE	SUPERLATIVE
1. long	*longer (than)*	*the longest (of all)*
2. small		
3. heavy		
4. comfortable		
5. hard		
6. difficult		
7. easy		
8. hot*		
9. cheap		
10. interesting		
11. pretty		
12. strong		
13. good		
14. bad		
15. far		

■ **EXERCISE 30:** Complete the sentences. Use the correct form of the ADJECTIVES in *italics*.

1. *large*   *The largest* _____ city in Canada is Toronto.

2. *long*   The Nile is _____ river in the world.

3. *interesting*   I'm taking four classes. My history class is _____

_____ of all.

4. *high*   Mt. McKinley in Alaska is _____
mountain in North America.

5. *tall*   The Sears Tower is _____ building in
Chicago.

_____

*Spelling note: If an adjective ends in one vowel and one consonant, double the consonant to form the superlative: *big-biggest, fat-fattest, thin-thinnest, hot-hottest.*

6. *big*   Lake Superior is _____ lake in North America.

7. *short*   February is _____ month of the year.

8. *far*   Pluto is _____ planet from the sun.

9. *beautiful*   In my opinion, Seattle is _____ city in the United States.

10. *bad*   In my opinion, Harry's Steak House is _____ restaurant in the city.

11. *good*   In my opinion, the Doghouse Cafe has _____ food in the city.

12. *comfortable*   Ken is sitting in _____ chair in the room.

13. *fast*   _____ way to travel is by airplane.

14. *good*   When you feel depressed, laughter is _____ medicine.

15. *large*   Asia is _____ continent in the world.

16. *small*   Australia is _____ continent in the world.

17. *expensive*   Sally ordered _____ food on the menu for dinner last night.

18. *easy*   Taking a taxi is _____ way to get to the airport.

19. *important*   I think good health is _____ thing in life.

20. *famous*   The Gateway Arch is _____ landmark in St. Louis, Missouri.

■ **EXERCISE 31:** Make at least four statements of COMPARISON about each group of pictures.

A. COMPARE THE SIZES OF THE THREE BALLS.

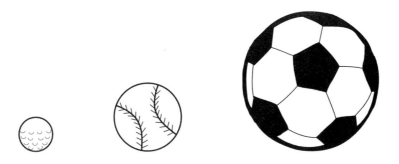

1. The golf ball is _____*smaller than*_____ the baseball.

2. The soccer ball is _____ the baseball.

3. The soccer ball is _____ of all.

4. The baseball isn't _____ as the soccer ball.

B. COMPARE THE AGES OF THE CHILDREN.

TOMMY
(3 years old)

HELEN
(6 years old)

ANN
(8 years old)

5. Ann is _____ Helen.

6. Tommy is _____ Helen and Ann.

7. Ann is _____ of all.

8. Helen isn't _____ as Ann.

C. COMPARE THE HEIGHTS OF THE THREE WOMEN.

LINDA   KAREN   ALICE

9. _____ is the tallest

10. _____ is the shortest.

11. _____ is taller than _____ but

shorter than _____.

12. _____ isn't as tall as _____.

D. COMPARE THE STRENGTH OF THE THREE MEN.

MIKE   JOE   DON

13. _____

14. _____

15. _____

16. _____

E. COMPARE THE PRICES OF THE THREE VEHICLES.

17. _____

18. _____

19. _____

20. _____

F. COMPARE HOW GOOD THE THREE TEST PAPERS ARE.

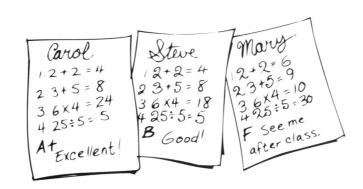

21. _____

22. _____

23. _____

24. _____

G. COMPARE HOW INTERESTING (TO YOU) THE THREE BOOKS LOOK.

25. _____

26. _____

27. _____

28. _____

■ **EXERCISE 32:**   Complete the sentences. Use the correct form (comparative or superlative) of the ADJECTIVES in *italics*.

1. *long*   The Yangtze River is _____ the Mississippi River.

2. *long*   The Nile is _____ river in the world.

3. *large*   The Caribbean Sea is _____ the Mediterranean Sea.

4. *large*   The Caribbean Sea is _____ sea in the world.

5. *high*   Mt. Everest is _____ mountain in the world.

6. *high*   Mt. Everest is _____ Mt. McKinley.

7. *big*   Africa is _____ North America.

8. *small*   Europe is _____ South America.

9. *large*   Asia is _____ continent in the world.

10. *big*   Canada is _____ the United States in area.

11. *large*   Indonesia is _____ Japan in population.

12. *good*   Fruit is _____ for your health

_____ candy.

13. *good*   The student cafeteria has _____ roast
beef sandwiches in the city.

14. *comfortable*   I have a pair of boots, a pair of sandals, and a pair of running

shoes. The sandals are _____

the boots, but the running shoes are _____

_____ of all.

15. *easy*   This exercise is _____ that one. This is

one of _____ exercises in the book.

16. *bad*   There are over 800 million people in the world who don't get to

eat. With few exceptions, poverty and hunger are _____
in rural areas than in cities and towns.

9-8 USING *ONE OF* + SUPERLATIVE + PLURAL NOUN

(a) The Amazon is **one of the longest rivers** in the world.	The superlative often follows **one of**. Notice the pattern:
(b) A Rolls Royce is **one of the most expensive cars** in the world.	**one of** + *superlative* + *plural noun*
(c) Alice is **one of the most intelligent people** in our class.	See Chart 8-5 for more information about **one of**.

■ **EXERCISE 33:** Make sentences about the following. Use **one of** + *superlative* + *plural noun*.

1. a high mountain in the world
   → *Mt. McKinley is one of the highest mountains in the world.*

2. a pretty park in *(this city)*
   → *Forest Park is one of the prettiest parks in St. Louis.*

3. a tall person in our class
   → *Talal is one of the tallest people★ in our class.*

4. a big city in the world

5. a beautiful place in the world

6. a nice person in our class

7. a long river in the world

_____
★*People* is usually used instead of **persons** in the plural.

8. a good restaurant in *(this city)*

9. a famous landmark in the world

10. an important event in the history of the world

■ **EXERCISE 34—WRITTEN:** Make sentences using *one of* + *superlative* + *plural noun.*

Example: a big city in Canada
Written: Montreal is one of the biggest cities in Canada.

1. a big city in Asia

2. a large state in the U.S.

3. a beautiful city in the world

4. a friendly person in our class

5. a good place to visit in the world

6. a famous person in the world

7. an important thing in life

8. a bad restaurant in *(this city)*

9. a famous landmark in *(name of a country)*

10. a tall building in *(this city)*

11. a dangerous sport in the world

12. a serious problem in the world

■ **EXERCISE 35—ORAL:** Discuss the questions.

1. How many brothers and sisters do you have? Are you the oldest?
2. Who is one of the most famous movie stars in the world?
3. In your opinion, what is the most exciting sport?
4. What is one of the most interesting experiences in your life?
5. In your opinion, what is the most beautiful place in the world?
6. What is one of the most important inventions in the modern world?
7. What is one of the worst experiences of your life?
8. What are the best things in life?
9. What was the happiest day of your life — or one of the happiest days of your life?
10. Who are the most important people in your life today?

■ **EXERCISE 36:** Take this quiz. If you don't know an answer, guess. After you take the quiz, form small groups to discuss the answers. You can figure out the correct answers by looking at the Table of Statistics on page 410.

PART I
1. What is the longest river in the world?
   A. the Yangtze
   B. the Amazon
   C. the Nile
   D. the Mississippi

2. Is the Amazon River longer than the Mississippi River?
   A. yes
   B. no

3. Is the Yangtze River longer than the Mississippi River?
   A. yes
   B. no

4. Is the Yangtze River as long as the Nile River?
   A. yes
   B. no

5. Which two rivers are almost the same length?
   A. the Nile and the Amazon
   B. the Amazon and the Yangtze
   C. the Nile and the Mississippi
   D. the Mississippi and the Amazon

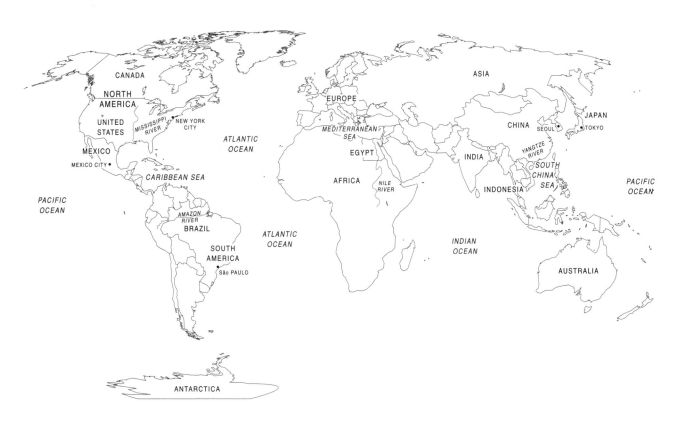

PART II

6. What is the largest sea in the world?
   A. the Mediterranean Sea
   B. the South China Sea
   C. the Caribbean Sea

7. Is the South China Sea the smallest of the three seas listed above?
   A. yes
   B. no

PART III

8. What is the deepest ocean in the world?
   A. the Atlantic Ocean
   B. the Indian Ocean
   C. the Pacific Ocean

9. Is the Indian Ocean larger than the Atlantic Ocean?
   A. yes
   B. no

PART IV

10. Below is a list of the continents in the world. List them in order according to size, from the largest to the smallest.

Africa	*Europe*
✔ *Antarctica*	*North America*
Asia	*South America*
Australia	

(1) _____ (the largest)

(2) _____

(3) _____

(4) _____

(5) ____*Antarctica*____

(6) _____

(7) _____ (the smallest)

PART V

11. Which of the following cities is the largest in population in the world?
    A. New York City, U.S.A.
    B. Seoul, Korea
    C. Mexico City, Mexico
    D. Tokyo, Japan

12. Is the population of Sao Paulo, Brazil, larger than the population of New York City, U.S.A.?
    A. yes
    B. no

13. Is the population of Sao Paulo, Brazil, larger than the population of Seoul, Korea?
    A. yes
    B. no

14. What is the largest city in North America?
    A. Mexico City
    B. New York City

PART VI

15. Which of the following countries is the largest in area in the world?
    A. Canada
    B. China
    C. the United States
    D. Brazil

16. Which of the following two countries is larger in area?
    A. Canada
    B. Brazil

17. Which of the following countries is the largest in population in the world?
    A. India
    B. China
    C. the United States
    D. Indonesia

18. Which of the following two countries is larger in population?
    A. India
    B. Indonesia

19. Which of the following two countries is larger in population?
    A. the United States
    B. Brazil

20. Which of the following two countries is smaller in population?
    A. Egypt
    B. Japan

TABLE OF STATISTICS

PART I

RIVER	LENGTH
the Amazon River	3,915 miles
the Mississippi River	2,348 miles
the Nile River	4,145 miles
the Yangtze River	3,900 miles

PART II

SEA	SIZE
the Caribbean Sea	970,000 square miles
the Mediterranean Sea	969,000 square miles
the South China Sea	895,000 square miles

PART III

OCEAN	SIZE	AVERAGE DEPTH
Atlantic Ocean	33,420,000 square feet	11,730 feet
Indian Ocean	28,350,500 square feet	12,598 feet
Pacific Ocean	64,186,300 square feet	12,925 feet

PART IV

CONTINENT	SIZE
Africa	11,707,000 square miles
Antarctica	5,500,000 square miles
Asia	17,129,000 square miles
Australia	2,942,000 square miles
Europe	4,057,000 square miles
North America	9,363,000 square miles
South America	6,886,000 square miles

PART V

CITY	POPULATION*
Mexico City, Mexico	28 million
New York, U.S.A.	15 million
Sao Paulo, Brazil	25 million
Seoul, Korea	22 million
Tokyo, Japan	30 million

PART VI

COUNTRY	AREA	POPULATION*
Brazil	3,286,470 sq mi	180 million
Canada	3,851,809 sq mi	29 million
China	3,691,000 sq mi	1,250 million **
Egypt	386,650 sq mi	65 million
India	1,269,339 sq mi	960 million
Indonesia	788,430 sq mi	205 million
Japan	145,740 sq mi	128 million
the United States	3,615,123 sq mi	268 million

* Approximate population in the year 2000.

** *1,250 million* is said as "one billion, two hundred fifty million." (It can also be said as "one thousand, two hundred and fifty million" in old-fashioned British English.)

9-9 ADJECTIVES AND ADVERBS

	ADJECTIVE	ADVERB	
(a) Ann is a *adjective* **careful** driver.	**careful** **slow** **quick** **easy**	**carefully** **slowly** **quickly** **easily**	An adjective describes a noun. In (a): **careful** describes **driver**. An adverb describes the action of a verb. In (b): **carefully** describes **drives**. Most adverbs are formed by adding **-ly** to an adjective.
(b) Ann drives *adverb* **carefully**.			
(c) John is a *adjective* **fast** driver.	**fast** **hard** **early** **late**	**fast** **hard** **early** **late**	The adjective form and the adverb form are the same for **fast**, **hard**, **early**, **late**.
(d) John drives *adverb* **fast**.			
(e) Linda is a *adjective* **good** writer.	**good**	**well**	**Well** is the adverb form of **good**.★
(f) Linda writes *adverb* **well**.			

★**Well** can also be used as an adjective to mean "not sick." *Paul was sick last week, but now he's well.*

■ **EXERCISE 37:** Complete the sentences by using the ADJECTIVE or ADVERB in *italics*.

1. *quiet, quietly* My hometown is small and _____quiet_____.

2. *quiet, quietly* Mr. Wilson whispered. He spoke _____quietly_____.

3. *clear, clearly* Anna pronounces every word _____.

4. *clear, clearly* We like to go boating in _____ weather.

5. *careless, carelessly* Boris makes a lot of mistakes when he writes. He's a

_____ writer.

6. *careless, carelessly* Boris writes _____.

7. *easy, easily* The teacher asked an _____ question.

8. *easy, easily* I answered the teacher's question _____.

9. *good, well* You speak English very _____.

10. *good, well* Your English is very _____.

■ **EXERCISE 38:** Complete the sentences by using the correct form (ADJECTIVE or ADVERB) of the word in *italics*.

1. *careful*   Do you drive _____?

2. *correct*   Carmen gave the _____ answer to the question.

3. *correct*   She answered the question _____.

4. *fast*   Mike is a _____ reader.

5. *quick*   Mike reads _____.

6. *fast*   Mike reads _____.

7. *neat*   Barbara has _____ handwriting. It is easy to read what she writes.

8. *neat*   Barbara writes _____.

9. *hard*   I study _____.

10. *hard*   The students took a _____ test.

11. *honest*   Roberto answered the question _____.

12. *slow*   Karen and Fumiko walked through the park _____.

13. *careless*   I made some _____ mistakes in my last composition.

14. *quick*   We were in a hurry, so we ate lunch _____.

15. *early*   Last night we had dinner _____ because we had to leave for the theater at 6:00.

16. *early*   We had an _____ dinner last night.

17. *good*   Jake has poor eyesight. He can't see

                 _____ without his glasses.

18. *good*   David is kind, generous, and thoughtful. He is a

                 _____ person.

19. *loud*   I speak _____ when I talk to my grandfather because he has trouble hearing.

20. *slow, clear*   Kim speaks English _____ and _____.

■ **EXERCISE 39:** Complete the sentences by using the correct form (ADJECTIVE or ADVERB) of the word in *italics*.

1. *good*   Did you sleep _____ last night?

2. *fast*   Anita is a _____ learner.

3. *quick*   She learns everything _____.

4. *fast*   Ahmed walks too _____. I can't keep up with him.

5. *soft*   Please speak _____. The children are asleep.

6. *easy*   This is an _____ exercise.

7. *hard*   It rained _____ yesterday.

8. *clear*   Our teacher explains everything _____.

9. *late*   Spiro came to class _____ yesterday.

10. *safe*   The plane arrived at the airport _____.

11. *hard*   Ms. Chan is a _____ worker.

12. *hard*   She works _____.

13. *late*   I paid my telephone bill _____.

14. *easy*   Ron lifted the heavy box _____. He's very strong.

15. *quiet*   Olga entered the classroom _____ because she was late for class.

16. *fast*   Mike talks too _____. I can't understand him.

17. *honest*   Shelley is an _____ person. I trust her completely.

18. *honest*   She speaks _____.

19. *good*   I didn't understand the teacher's explanation very _____.

20. *good*   We had a _____ time at the party last night.

21. *good*   Linda speaks _____, but she doesn't write

_____.

22. *fluent*   Nadia speaks French _____.

9-10 MAKING COMPARISONS WITH ADVERBS

		COMPARATIVE	SUPERLATIVE	
(a)	Kim speaks **more fluently than** Ali (does). (b) Anna speaks **the most fluently of all**.	**more fluently** **more slowly** **more quickly**	**the most fluently** **the most slowly** **the most quickly**	Use **more** and **most** with adverbs that end in **-ly**.★
(c)	Mike worked **harder than** Sam (did). (d) Sue worked **the hardest of all**.	**harder** **faster** **earlier** **later**	**the hardest** **the fastest** **the earliest** **the latest**	Use **-er** and **-est** with irregular adverbs: **hard, fast, early, late**.
(e)	Rosa writes **better than** I do. (f) Kim writes **the best of all**.	**better**	**the best**	**Better** and **best** are forms of the adverb *well*.

★Exception: *early–earlier–earliest*.

■ **EXERCISE 40:**   Complete the sentences by using the correct form (COMPARATIVE or SUPERLATIVE) of the ADVERBS in *italics*.

1. *late*   Karen got home ___*later than*___ Alice (did).

2. *quickly*   I finished my work _____ Tom (did).

3. *beautifully*   Gina sings _____ Susan (does).

4. *beautifully*   Ann sings _____ of all.

5. *hard*   My sister works _____ I (do).

6. *hard*   My brother works _____ of all.

7. *carefully*   My husband drives _____ I (do).

8. *early*   We arrived at the party _____ the Smiths (did).

9. *early*   The Wilsons arrived at the party _____ of all.

10. *well*   You can write _____ I (can).

11. *well*   Ken can write _____ of all.

12. *clearly*   Anita pronounces her words _____ Tina (does).

13. *fast*   I work _____ Jim (does).

14. *fast*   Toshi finished his work _____ of all.

15. *loudly*   Ali speaks _____ Yoko (does.)

16. *fluently*   Sue speaks Spanish _____ I (do).

17. *fluently*   Ted speaks Spanish _____ of all.

18. *slowly*   A snail moves _____ a crab (does).

■ **EXERCISE 41:**   Use the correct form (ADJECTIVE or ADVERB, COMPARATIVE or SUPERLATIVE) of the words in *italics*.

1. *careful*   Karen drives _____ *more carefully than* _____ her brother does.

2. *beautiful*   A tiger is _____ a goat.

3. *neat*   Paul's apartment is _____ mine.

4. *neat*   Peter's apartment is _____ of all.

5. *neat*   You write _____ I do.

6. *neat*   Ann writes _____ of all.

7. *heavy*   This suitcase is _____ that one.

8. *clear*   This author explains her ideas _____ that author.

9. *good*   I like rock music _____ classical music.

10. *good*   My husband can sing _____ I can.

11. *good*   My daughter can sing _____ of all.

12. *hard*   Sue studies _____ Fred.

13. *hard*   Jean studies _____ of all.

14. *long*   Almost universally, wives work _____
hours than their husbands because women take primary responsibility
for household chores and child-rearing.

15. *late*   Robert usually goes to bed _____
his roommate.

16. *clear*   Anna pronounces her words _____
of all the students in the class.

17. *sharp*   A razor is usually _____ a kitchen knife.

18. *artistic*   My son is _____ my daughter.

19. *slow*   I eat _____ my husband does.

20. *dangerous*   A motorcycle is _____ a bicycle.

9-11 USING *AS . . . AS* WITH ADVERBS

(a) Bob doesn't study **as hard as** his brother (does). (b) I didn't finish my work **as quickly as** Sue (did). (c) Yoko can speak English **as well as** Tony (can).	Notice the pattern in the examples: **as** + *adverb* + **as**
(d) I'm working **as fast as I can**. (e) I'm working **as fast as possible**. (f) Alex came **as quickly as he could**. (g) Alex came **as quickly as possible**.	Notice the patterns in the examples: **as** + *adverb* + **as** is frequently followed by *subject* + **can**/**could** or by **possible**.

■ **EXERCISE 42:**   Complete the sentences. Compare John to your classmates or yourself.

1. John is lazy. He doesn't work as hard _____ *as Yoko (does). / as I (do).* _____

2. John is a reckless driver. He doesn't drive as carefully _____

3. I can't read John's handwriting. He doesn't write as neatly _____

4. John goes to bed late. He doesn't go to bed as early _____

5. John was the last person to finish the test. He didn't finish it as quickly

_____

6. John speaks softly. He doesn't speak as loudly _____

7. John is never in a hurry. He takes his time. He doesn't walk as fast _____

8. John is an insomniac. He doesn't sleep as well _____

9. John rarely studies. He doesn't study as hard _____

■ **EXERCISE 43—ORAL:** Change the sentences by using *as . . . as* + *possible* or *can/could.*

Example: Please come early.
Response: Please come as early as possible. / Please come as early as you can.

Example: (. . .) walked fast.
Response: Surasuk walked as fast as possible. / Surasuk walked as fast as he could.

1. Please come quickly.
2. (. . .) came quickly.
3. Please write neatly.
4. I opened the door quietly.
5. Please come soon.
6. (. . .) came soon.
7. Pronounce each word clearly.
8. Do you study hard?
9. When (. . .) saw a mean dog, he/she ran home fast.
10. I write to my parents often.
11. (. . .) is working fast.
12. Please give me your homework soon.
13. I'll get home early.
14. (. . .) answered the question well.
15. I'll call you soon.
16. (. . .) goes swimming often.
17. Please finish the test soon.
18. I'll pay my telephone bill soon.

■ **EXERCISE 44—REVIEW:** Choose the correct completion.

1. A lion is _____ a tiger.
   A. similar   B. similar with   C. similar from   D. similar to

2. Lions and tigers are _____.
   A. the same   B. similar   C. similar to   D. the same as

3. Good health is one of _____ in a person's life.
   A. best thing   C. the best things
   B. the best thing   D. best things

4. There were many chairs in the room. I sat in _____ chair.
   A. the comfortablest   C. most comfortable
   B. the most comfortable   D. more comfortable

5. Jane's story was _____ Jack's story.
   A. funnier than
   B. funny than
   C. more funnier than
   D. more funny

6. My last name is _____ my cousin's.
   A. same   B. same from   C. same as   D. the same as

7. I live _____ away from school than you do.
   A. far   B. farther   C. more far   D. farthest

8. Ali speaks _____ than Hamid.
   A. more clearly
   B. clearlier
   C. more clear
   D. more clearer

9. The weather in Canada _____ the weather in Mexico.
   A. is less hot than
   B. isn't as hot as
   C. is hotter
   D. isn't hot

10. Robert works hard every day, but his brother _____.
   A. is   B. isn't   C. does   D. doesn't

■ **EXERCISE 45—ERROR ANALYSIS:** Find and correct the mistakes in the following sentences.

1. Your pen is alike mine.

2. Kim's coat is similar with mine.

3. Jack's coat is same mine.

4. Soccer balls are different with basketballs.

5. Soccer is one of most popular sports in the world.

6. Green sea turtles live more long from elephants.

7. My grade on the test was worst from yours. You got a more better grade.

8. A monkey is intelligenter than a turtle.

9. Africa isn't as large than Asia.

10. Pedro speaks English more fluent than Ernesto.

11. The exploding human population is the most great threat to all forms of life on earth.

12. The Mongol Empire was the bigger land empire in the entire history of the world.

■ **EXERCISE 46—ORAL REVIEW (BOOKS CLOSED):** Pair up with a classmate.
   STUDENT A: Your book is open.
   STUDENT B: Your book is closed. Respond in complete sentences.

   1. What's the longest river in the world?
   2. What's the biggest continent? What's the second biggest continent?
   3. What country has the largest population?
   4. Is a square the same as a rectangle?
   5. Name a country that is farther south than Mexico.
   6. Name an animal that is similar to a horse.
   7. Name a place that is noisier than a library.
   8. Is a dormitory like an apartment building? How are they different? How are they similar?
   9. Is (. . .)'s grammar book different from yours?
   10. What is one of the most famous landmarks in the world?

   Switch roles.
   11. Is the population of Seoul, Korea, larger or smaller than the population of Sao Paulo, Brazil?
   12. Is the Atlantic Ocean deeper than the Indian Ocean?
   13. What's the smallest continent in the world?
   14. Name two students in this class who speak the same native language. Do they come from the same country?
   15. Look at (. . .) and (. . .). How are they different?
   16. Is a lake like a river? How are they different? How are they similar?
   17. Name an insect that is smaller than a bee.
   18. Name a city that is farther north than Rome, Italy.
   19. What is the most popular sport in your country?
   20. What is one of the most important inventions in the modern world? Why is it more important than *(name of another invention)*.

■ **EXERCISE 47—REVIEW:** Write about or talk about things and people in this room. Orally or in writing, compare things and people you see in the classroom right now. Look at this thing and that thing, and then compare them. Look at this person and that person, and then compare them.

■ **EXERCISE 48—REVIEW:** Write about one or more of the following topics.

   1. Write about your family. Compare the members of your family. Include yourself in the comparisons. (Who is younger than you? Who is the youngest of all? Etc.)
   2. Write about your childhood friends when you were ten years old. Compare them. Include yourself in the comparisons. (Who could run faster than you? Who could run the fastest of all? Etc.)
   3. What are your three favorite places in the world? Why? Compare them.
   4. What are the roles of health, money, and love in your life? Compare them.

CHAPTER 10
Expressing Ideas with Verbs

10-1 USING *SHOULD*

(a) My clothes are dirty. **I should wash** them. (b) Tom is sleepy. He **should go** to bed. (c) You're sick. You **should see** a doctor.	**Should** means "This is a good idea. This is good advice."
(d) I You She He } **should go**. It We They	**Should** is followed by the simple form of a verb. INCORRECT: *He should goes.* INCORRECT: *He should to go.*
(e) You **should not leave** your grammar book at home. You need it in class. (f) You **shouldn't leave** your grammar book at home.	NEGATIVE: *should not* CONTRACTION: *should + not = shouldn't*

■ **EXERCISE 1:** Complete the sentences. Begin the sentences with "**You should . . . .**" Use the expressions in the list or your own words.

buy a new pair of shoes call the landlady go to the bank go to the immigration office	✔ go to the post office go to bed and take a nap see a dentist study harder

1. A: I want to mail a package.

   B: *You should go to the post office.*

2. A: I'm sleepy.

   B: _____

3. A: I need to cash a check.

   B: _____

4. A: I have a toothache.

   B: _____

5. A: I'm flunking all of my courses at school.

   B: _____

6. A: The plumbing in my apartment doesn't work.

   B: _____

7. A: I need to renew my visa.

   B: _____

8. A: My shoes have holes in the bottom.

   B: _____

■ **EXERCISE 2:**   Complete the sentences. Use **should** or **shouldn't**.

1. Students ____*should*____ come to class every day.

2. Students ____*shouldn't*____ cut class.

3. We _____ waste our money on things we don't need.

4. It's raining. You _____ take your umbrella when you leave.

5. Jimmy, you _____ pull the cat's tail!

6. People _____ be cruel to animals.

7. Your plane leaves at 8:00. You _____ get to the airport by 7:00.

8. Life is short. We _____ waste it.

9. You _____ smoke in a public place because the smoke bothers other people.

10. We _____ cross a street at an intersection. We

_____ jaywalk.

11. When you go to New York City, you _____ see a play on Broadway.

12. You _____ walk alone on city streets after midnight. It's dangerous.

13. When you go to Bangkok, you _____ visit the Floating Market.

14. When you go to a football game, you _____ throw things on the field.

■ **EXERCISE 3—ORAL:** In groups of four, give advice using *should* and *shouldn't*.
Student A should request advice first, then Student B, etc.

1. STUDENT A: English is not my native language. What advice can you give me about good ways to learn English?
2. STUDENT B: I am a teenager. What advice can you give me about being a good person and living a happy life?
3. STUDENT C: I am a newcomer. What advice can you give me about going to this school and living in this city?
4. STUDENT D: I have a job interview tomorrow. What advice can you give me about going to a job interview?

■ **EXERCISE 4—WRITTEN:** Write about your hometown. Use a separate piece of paper.

I'm a tourist. I'm going to visit your hometown. Is your hometown a good place for a tourist to visit? Why? What should I do when I'm there? Where should I go? What should I see? What shouldn't I do? Are there places I shouldn't visit? Will I enjoy my visit? Write a composition in which you tell me (a tourist) about your hometown.

10-2 USING *LET'S*

(a) Bob: What should we do tonight? Ann: **Let's go to a movie**. Bob: Okay. (b) Sue: I'm tired. Don: I'm tired, too. **Let's take a break**. Sue: That's a good idea!	*Let's (do something) = I have a suggestion for you and me. (let's = let us)* In (a): *Let's go to a movie = I think we should go to a movie. Do you want to go to a movie?*

■ **EXERCISE 5:** Complete the dialogues. Use *let's*. Use the expressions in the list or your own words.

eat	go to a seafood restaurant
get a cup of coffee	go to the zoo
go dancing	✔ leave at six-thirty
go to Florida	walk
go to a movie	

1. A: What time should we leave for the airport?

   B: ___*Let's leave at six-thirty.*_____

   A: Okay.

2. A: Where should we go for our vacation?

   B: _____

   A: That's a good idea.

3. A: Where do you want to go for dinner tonight?

   B: _____

4. A: The weather is beautiful today. _____

   B: Okay. Great!

5. A: I'm bored. _____

   B: I can't. I have to study.

6. A: Should we take the bus downtown or walk downtown?

   B: It's a nice day. _____

7. A: Dinner's ready! The food's on the table!

   B: Great! _____ I'm starving!

8. A: Where should we go Saturday night?

   B: _____
   A: Good idea!

9. A: We have an hour between classes. _____
   B: Okay. That sounds like a good idea.

■ **EXERCISE 6—ORAL:**   Pair up with a classmate. Practice using *let's*.
    STUDENT A: Your book is open. Say the words in the book.
    STUDENT B: Your book is closed. Use *let's* in your response.
    STUDENT A: Respond to Student B's suggestion.

    Example: It's a beautiful day today. What should we do?
    STUDENT A: It's a beautiful day today. What should we do?
    STUDENT B: Let's go to Woodland Park Zoo.
    STUDENT A: Great! What a good idea! Let's go!

1. What time should we go out to dinner tonight?
2. When should we go to *(name of a place)?*
3. What should we do this evening?
4. I want to do something fun tomorrow.

Switch roles.
5. What should we do tomorrow? It's a holiday, and we don't have to go to class.
6. I'm bored. Think of something we can do.
7. My plane leaves at six. What time should we leave for the airport?
8. It's *(name of a classmate)*'s birthday tomorrow. Should we do something special for him/her?

10-3   USING *HAVE* + INFINITIVE (*HAS TO / HAVE TO*)

(a) People **need to eat** food. (b) People **have to eat** food. (c) Jack **needs to study** for his test. (d) Jack **has to study** for his test.	(a) and (b) have basically the same meaning. (c) and (d) have basically the same meaning. ***Have*** + *infinitive* has a special meaning: it expresses the same idea as ***need***.
(e) I **had to study** last night.	PAST FORM: ***had*** + *infinitive*.
(f) **Do** you **have to** leave now? (g) What time **does** Jim **have to** leave? (h) Why **did** they **have to** leave yesterday?	QUESTION FORM: ***do***, ***does***, or ***did*** is used in questions with ***have to***.
(i) I **don't have to** study tonight. (j) The concert was free. We **didn't have to** buy tickets.	NEGATIVE FORM: ***do***, ***does***, or ***did*** is used with ***have to*** in the negative.

■ **EXERCISE 7—ORAL:**   Answer the questions.

1. What do you want to do today?
2. What do you have to do today?
3. What do you want to do tomorrow?
4. What do you have to do tomorrow?
5. What does a student need to do or have to do?
6. Who has to go shopping? Why?
7. Who has to go to the post office? Why?
8. Who has to go to the bank? Why?
9. Where do you have to go today? Why?
10. Where do you want to go tomorrow? Why?
11. What did you have to do yesterday? Why?
12. Did you have responsibilities at home when you were a child? What did you have to do?
11. If you're driving a car and the traffic light turns red, what do you have to do?
12. What do you have to do before you cross a busy street?
13. Do you have to learn English? Why?
14. Who has a job? What are some of the things you have to do when you're at work?
15. What kind of job did you have in the past? What did you have to do when you had that job?

■ **EXERCISE 8—ORAL (BOOKS CLOSED):**   Use *have to/has to*. Use *because*.

Example: go downtown / buy some new shoes
STUDENT A: I have to go downtown because I have to buy some new shoes.
TEACHER: Why does (Student A) have to go downtown?
STUDENT B: (Student A) has to go downtown because he/she has to buy some new shoes.

1. go to the drugstore / buy some toothpaste
2. go to the grocery store / get some milk
3. go shopping / get a new coat
4. go to the post office / mail a package
5. stay home tonight / study grammar
6. go to the hospital / visit a friend
7. go to the bank / cash a check
8. go downtown / go to the immigration office
9. go to the bookstore / buy a notebook
10. go to *(name of a store in the city)* / buy *(a particular thing at that store)*

■ **EXERCISE 9:** Complete the sentences. Use the words in parentheses. Use a form of **has/have** + *infinitive* in all the completions.

1. A: Jack can't join us for dinner tonight.
   B: Why not?

   A: *(he, work)* ___He has to work___.

   B: *(he, work)* ___Does he have to work___ tomorrow night too? If he doesn't, maybe we should postpone the dinner until then.

2. A: Why *(you, go)* _____ to the library later tonight?

   B: *(I, find)* _____ some information for my research paper.

3. A: It's almost four-thirty. What time *(Sue, leave for)* _____ the airport?

   B: Around five. *(she, be)* _____ at the airport at six-fifteen.

4. A: Why did you go to the bookstore after class yesterday?

   B: *(I, buy)* _____ some colored pencils.

   A: Oh? Why *(you, buy)* _____ colored pencils?
   B: I need them for some drawings I plan to do for my botany class.

5. A: *(I, go)* _____ to the store.
   B: Why?

   A: Because *(I, get)* _____ some rice and fresh fruit.

6. A: Kate didn't come to the movie with us last night.
   B: Why?

   A: Because *(she, study)* _____ for a test.

7. A: What time *(you, be)* _____ at the dentist's office?
   B: Three. I have a three o'clock appointment.

8. A: *(Tom, find)* _____ a new apartment?
   B: Yes, he does. He can't stay in his present apartment.

9. A: *(Yoko, not, take)* _____ another English course. Her English is very good.

   B: *(you, take)* _____ another English course?
   A: Yes, I do. I need to study more English.

10. A: Was Steve at home yesterday evening?

   B: No. *(he, stay)* _____ late at the office.
   B: Why?

   A: *(he, finish)* _____ a report for his boss.

10-4 USING *MUST*

(a) People need food. People ***have to eat*** food. (b) People need food. People ***must eat*** food.	(a) and (b) have the same meaning: *must eat = have to eat*
(c) *I* *You* *She* *He* } ***must work***. *It* *We* *They*	***Must*** is followed by the simple form of a verb. INCORRECT: *He must works.* INCORRECT: *He must to work.*
(d) You ***must not be*** late for work if you want to keep your job.	***must not*** = Don't do this! You don't have a choice.
(e) You ***don't have to go*** to the movie with us if you don't want to.	***don't have to*** = It's not necessary, but you have a choice.

Compare the following examples. Notice the difference between ***should*** and ***must***.

MUST	SHOULD
SOMETHING IS VERY IMPORTANT. SOMETHING IS NECESSARY. YOU DO NOT HAVE A CHOICE.	SOMETHING IS A GOOD IDEA, BUT YOU HAVE A CHOICE.
(f) I ***must study*** tonight. I'm going to take a very important test tomorrow.	(g) I ***should study*** tonight. I have some homework to do, but I'm tired. I'll study tomorrow night. I'm going to go to bed now.
(h) You ***must take*** an English course. You cannot graduate without it.	(i) You ***should take*** an English course. It will help you.
(j) Johnny, this is your mother speaking. You ***must eat*** your vegetables. You can't leave the table until you eat your vegetables.	(k) Johnny, you ***should eat*** your vegetables. They're good for you. You'll grow up to be strong and healthy.

■ **EXERCISE 10:** Complete the sentences. Use *must*. Use the expressions in the list.

> close the door behind you
> go to medical school
> ✔ have a driver's license
> have a library card
> have a passport
> listen to English on the radio and TV
> make new friends who speak English
>
> pay an income tax
> read English newspapers and magazines
> speak English outside of class every day
> stop
> study harder
> talk to myself in English
> take one pill every six hours

1. According to the law,* a driver _____*must have a driver's license.*_____

2. If a traffic light is red, a car _____

3. If you want to check a book out of the library, you _____

   _____

4. Nancy has a job in Chicago. She earns a good salary. According to the law, she

   _____

5. I failed the last two tests in my biology class. According to my professor, I

   _____

6. I want to travel abroad. According to the law, I _____

   _____

7. If you want to become a doctor, you _____

8. John's doctor gave him a prescription. According to

   the directions on the bottle, John _____

   _____

9. Jimmy ! It's cold outside. When you come inside, you _____

   _____

10. I want to improve my English. According to my teacher, I _____

   _____

---

*according to the law = the law says.

■ **EXERCISE 11—ORAL:** Answer the questions.

1. When must you have a passport?
2. If you live in an apartment, what is one thing you must do and one thing you must not do?
3. Name one thing a driver must do and one thing a driver must not do.
4. If you are on an airplane, what is one thing you must do and one thing you must not do?
5. Name something you must have a ticket for. Name something you don't have to have a ticket for.

■ **EXERCISE 12:** Choose the correct completion.

1. If you want to keep your job, you _____ be late for work. It is necessary for you to be on time.
   A. must not   B. don't have to   C. doesn't have to

2. My office is close enough to my apartment for me to walk to work. I _____ take a bus. I only take a bus in bad weather.
   A. must not   B. don't have to   C. doesn't have to

3. Some schools require schoolchildren to wear uniforms to school, but my children's

   school doesn't require uniforms. My children _____ wear uniforms to school.
   A. must not   B. don't have to   C. doesn't have to

4. Jimmy, it is very important to be careful with matches! You _____ play with matches.
   A. must not   B. don't have to   C. doesn't have to

5. Jack is twenty-four, but he still lives with his parents. That saves him a lot of money.

For example, he _____ pay rent or buy his own food.
    A. must not   B. don't have to   C. doesn't have to

6. The water in that river is badly polluted. You _____ drink it.
    A. must not   B. don't have to   C. doesn't have to _____

7. If you have a credit card, you _____ pay for a purchase in cash. You can charge it.
    A. must not   B. don't have to   C. doesn't have to

8. When an airplane is taking off, you have to be in your seat with your seat belt on.

You _____ stand up and walk around when an airplane is taking off.
    A. must not   B. don't have to   C. doesn't have to

10-5 MODAL AUXILIARIES

(a) Anita	*can* *couldn't* *may* *might* *must* *should* *will* go to class.	An auxiliary is a helping verb. It comes in front of the simple form of a main verb. The following helping verbs are called "modal auxiliaries": *can*, *could*, *may*, *might*, *must*, *should*, *will*, *would*. They are followed by the simple form of a verb (without *to*).
(b) Anita	*is able to* *is going to* *has to* go to class.	Expressions that are similar to modal auxiliaries are: *be able to*, *be going to*, *have to*.

■ **EXERCISE 13:** Add *to* where necessary. If *to* is not necessary, write "X."

1. My sister can _____X_____ play the guitar very well.

2. We have ____to____ pay our rent on the first of the month.

3. Could you please _____ open the window? Thanks.

4. I wasn't able _____ visit my friends yesterday because I was busy.

5. You shouldn't _____ drink twenty cups of coffee a day.

6. Will you _____ be at the meeting tomorrow?

7. Does everyone have _____ be at the meeting?

8. You must not _____ miss the meeting. It's important.

9. Jennifer might not _____ be there tomorrow.

10. May I _____ use your telephone?

11. We couldn't _____ go to the concert last night because we didn't have tickets.

12. Can you _____ play a musical instrument?

13. What time are you going _____ arrive?

14. It may _____ be too cold for us to go swimming tomorrow.

10-6 SUMMARY CHART: MODAL AUXILIARIES AND SIMILAR EXPRESSIONS

	AUXILIARY*	MEANING	EXAMPLE
(A)	*can*	ability	I *can* sing.
		polite question	*Can* you please help me?
(b)	*could*	past ability	I *couldn't* go to class yesterday.
		polite question	*Could* you please help me?
(c)	*may*	possibility	It *may* rain tomorrow.
		polite question	*May* I help you?
(d)	*might*	possibility	It *might* rain tomorrow.
(e)	*must*	necessity	You *must* have a passport.
(f)	*should*	advisability	You *should* see a doctor.
(g)	*will*	future happening	My sister *will* meet us at the airport.
(h)	*would*	polite question	*Would* you please open the door?
(i)	*be able to*	ability	I *wasn't able to* attend the meeting.
(j)	*be going to*	future happening	Tina *is going to* meet us at the airport.
(k)	*has / have to*	necessity	I *have to* study tonight.
(l)	*had to*	past necessity	I *had to* study last night too.

*See the following charts for more information: *can*, Charts 7-1 and 7-2; *could*, Chart 7-4; *may* and *might*, Chart 6-10; *must*, Chart 10-4; *should*, Chart 10-1; *will*, Charts 6-5, 6-6, and 6-10; *would*, Chart 7-14; *be able to*, Chart 7-12; *be going to*, Chart 6-1; *has/have/had to*, Chart 10-3.

■ **EXERCISE 14—ORAL:**   In small groups, give responses to the following. Each person in the group should give a different response.

> *Example:*   Name something you *had to* do yesterday.
> STUDENT A: I had to go to class.
> STUDENT B: I had to go to the post office to buy some stamps.
> STUDENT C: I had to study for a test.
> STUDENT D: Etc.

1. Name something you *can* do.
2. Name something you *couldn't* do yesterday.
3. Name something you *may* do tomorrow,
4. Name something you *might* do tomorrow.
5. Name something you *must* do this week.
6. Name something you *have to* do today.
7. Name something you *don't have to* do today.
8. Name something you *should* do this evening.
9. Name something you *will* do this evening.
10. Name something you *are going to* do this week.
11. Name something you *weren't able to* do when you were a child.
12. Name something you *had to* do when you were a child.
13. You want to borrow something from a classmate. Ask a polite question with ***could***.
14. You want a classmate to do something for you. Ask a polite question with ***would***.
15. A classmate has something that you want. Ask a polite question with ***may***.
16. Name something that *may* happen in the world in the next ten years.
17. Name something that (probably) *won't* happen in the world in the next ten years.
18. Name some things that this school *should* do or *shouldn't* do to make the school a better place for students.

■ **EXERCISE 15—ERROR ANALYSIS:**   Find and correct the mistakes in the following.

1. Would you please to help me?

2. I will can go to the meeting tomorrow.

3. Ken should writes us a letter.

4. I have to went to the store yesterday.

5. Susie! You must not to play with matches!

6. May you please hand me that book?

7. Ann couldn't answered my question.

8. Shelley can't goes to the concert tomorrow.

9. Let's to go to a movie tonight.

■ **EXERCISE 16—REVIEW OF VERBS:** Choose the correct completion.

1. Tom _____ every day.
   A. shaves   B. is shaving   C. has to shaves

2. _____ go to class every day?
   A. Are you   B. Do you have   C. Do you

3. Yoko _____ to be here tomorrow.
   A. will   B. may   C. is going

4. Jack _____ be in class yesterday.
   A. didn't   B. can't   C. couldn't

5. Fatima _____ to her sister on the phone yesterday.
   A. spoke   B. can speak   C. speaks

6. I _____ my rent last month.
   A. might pay   B. will pay   C. paid

7. Shh. Ken _____ on the phone right now.
   A. talks   B. can talk   C. is talking

8. I want to go to a movie tonight, but I _____ home and study.
   A. should stay   B. stayed   C. stay

9. We _____ to the zoo tomorrow.
   A. will going   B. might go   C. will can go

10. I _____ in class right now.
    A. sit   B. am sitting   C. sitting

PRESENT PROGRESSIVE (right now) (a) It's 10:00 now. Boris *is sitting* in class.	The present progressive describes an activity in progress right now, at the moment of speaking. See Chart 3-1. In (a): Right now it is 10:00. Boris began to sit before 10:00. Sitting is in progress at 10:00.
PAST PROGRESSIVE (in progress yesterday) (b) It was 10:00. Boris *was sitting* in class.	The past progressive describes an activity in progress at a particular time in the past. In (b): Boris began to sit in class before 10:00 yesterday. At 10:00 yesterday, sitting in class was in progress.

PRESENT PROGRESSIVE FORM: *AM, IS, ARE* + *-ING*
(c) It's 10:00.   I   *am sitting*   in class.
            Boris   *is sitting*   in class.
            We   *are sitting*   in class.
	The forms of the present progressive and the past progressive consist of *be* + *-ing*.
	The present progressive uses the present forms of *be*: *am*, *is*, and *are* + *-ing*.

PAST PROGRESSIVE FORM: *WAS, WERE* + *-ING* (d) It was 10:00. Boris *was sitting* in class. We *were sitting* in class.	The past progressive uses the past forms of *be*: *was* and *were* + *-ing*.

Boris *is sitting* in class right now at ten o'clock.

Boris *was sitting* in class yesterday at ten o'clock.

■ **EXERCISE 17:** Complete the sentences. Use a form of *be* + *sit*.

1. I _____*am sitting*_____ in class right now.

2. I _____*was sitting*_____ in class yesterday too.

3. You _____*are sitting*_____ in class right now.

4. You _____*were sitting*_____ in class yesterday too.

5. Tony _____*is sitting*_____ in class right now.

6. He _____*was sitting*_____ in class yesterday too.

7. We _____*are sitting*_____ in class today.

8. We _____*were sitting*_____ in class yesterday too.

9. Rita _____*is sitting*_____ in class now.

10. She _____*was sitting*_____ in class yesterday too.

11. Rita and Tony _____*are sitting*_____ in class today.

12. They _____*were sitting*_____ in class yesterday too.

■ **EXERCISE 18:** Use the words in parentheses to complete the sentences. Discuss the meaning of the phrase "in progress."

1. Paul started to eat dinner at 7:00. At 7:05, Mary came. Paul *(eat)* __*was*__ __*eating*__ when Mary *(come)* __*came*__ at 7:05.

2. Bobby was at home yesterday evening. His favorite program was on television last night. It started at 8:00. It ended at 9:00. At 8:30, his friend Kristin called. When Kristin *(call)* _called_ at 8:30, Bobby *(watch)* _was watching_ TV.

3. Rosa played her guitar for an hour yesterday morning. She started to play her guitar at 9:30. She stopped at 10:30. Mike arrived at her apartment at 10:00. At 10:00, Rosa *(play)* _was playing_ her guitar.

■ **EXERCISE 19—ORAL:** Look at the pictures. Use the PAST PROGRESSIVE to describe the activities that were in progress.

Mr. and Mrs. Gold invited several friends to their house for the weekend. A thief stole Mrs. Gold's jewelry at midnight on Saturday. What were the guests doing at midnight?

10-8 USING *WHILE* WITH THE PAST PROGRESSIVE

(a) The phone rang **while** *I was sleeping.* OR: (b) **While** *I was sleeping,* the phone rang.	**while** + *subject* + *verb* = *a time clause* *While I was sleeping* is a time clause. A *while*-clause describes an activity that was in progress at the time another activity happened. The verb in a *while*-clause is often past progressive (e.g., *was sleeping*).

■ **EXERCISE 20—ORAL:** Combine the sentences. Use **while**.

1. I was studying last night.
   Rita called.
   → *While I was studying last night, Rita called.*
   → *Rita called while I was studying last night.*

2. Someone knocked on my apartment door.
   I was eating breakfast yesterday morning.

3. I was cooking dinner yesterday evening.
   I burned my hand.

4. I was studying last night.
   A mouse suddenly appeared
   on my desk.

5. Yoko raised her hand.
   The teacher was talking.

6. A tree fell on my car.
   I was driving home yesterday.

10-9 *WHILE* vs. *WHEN* IN PAST TIME CLAUSES

(a) The mouse appeared *while* **I was studying.** OR: (b) *While* **I was studying,** the mouse appeared.	The verb in a *while*-clause is often past progressive, as in (a) and (b).
(c) *When the mouse* **appeared,** I was studying. OR: (d) I was studying *when the mouse* **appeared.**	The verb in a *when*-clause is often simple past, as in (c) and (d).

■ **EXERCISE 21:**   Complete the sentences. Use the PAST PROGRESSIVE in the ***while***-clauses.
Use the SIMPLE PAST in the ***when***-clauses.

1. While I *(wash)* _____*was washing*_____ dishes last night, I *(get)*

   _____*got*_____ a phone call from my best friend.

2. When my best friend *(call)* _____ last night, I *(wash)*

   _____ dishes.

3. My friend Jessica *(come)* _____ while I *(eat)*

   _____ dinner last night.

4. I *(eat)* _____ dinner when my friend Jessica *(come)*

   _____ last night.

5. Jason *(wear)* _____ a suit and tie when I *(see)*

   _____ him yesterday.

6. My roommate came home late last night. I *(sleep)* _____

   when she *(get)* _____ home.

7. When Gina *(call)* _____ last night, I *(take)*

   _____ a bubble bath.

8. While I *(watch)* _____ TV last night and *(relax)*

   _____ after a long day, my new puppy *(take)*

   _____ my wallet from my bedside table.

■ **EXERCISE 22—ORAL:** Perform and describe actions using **while**-clauses or **when**-clauses.

STUDENT A: Perform your action. Use the PRESENT PROGRESSIVE to describe what you are doing. Continue to perform the action.

STUDENT B: Perform your action, then stop.

STUDENT A: After Student B stops, you stop too.

Example: A: erase the board
              B: open the door

TEACHER: (Student A), what are you doing?

STUDENT A: I'm erasing the board right now.

TEACHER: (Student B), would you please open the door?

STUDENT B: *(Student B opens the door.)*

TEACHER: Thank you. You may both sit down again. (Student C), will you please describe the two actions we saw?

STUDENT C: While (Student A) was erasing the board, (Student B) opened the door. OR: (Student A) was erasing the board when (Student B) opened the door.

1. A: Write on the board.
   B: Drop a book on the floor.
2. A: Walk around the room.
   B: Say hello to (Student A).
3. A: Look out the window.
   B: Take (Student A)'s grammar book.
4. A: Draw a picture on the board.
   B: Ask (Student A) a question.

10-10 SIMPLE PAST vs. PAST PROGRESSIVE

(a) Jane **called** me yesterday. (b) I **talked** to Jane for an hour last night. (c) We **went** to Jack's house last Friday. (d) What time **did** you **get up** this morning?	The **simple past** describes activities or situations that began and ended at a particular time in the past (e.g., *yesterday, last night*).
(e) I **was studying** when Jane called me yesterday. (f) While I **was studying** last night, Jane called.	The **past progressive** describes an activity that was in progress (was happening) at the time another action happened. In (e) and (f): The studying was in progress when Jane called.
(g) I **opened** my umbrella when it **began** to rain.	If both the *when*-clause and the main clause in a sentence are simple past, it means that the action in the *when*-clause happened first and the action in the main clause happened second. In (g): First, it began to rain; second, I opened my umbrella.
COMPARE (h) When the phone **rang**, I **answered** it. (i) When the phone **rang**, I **was studying**.	In (h): First, the phone rang; second, I answered it. In (i): First, the studying was in progress; second, the phone rang.

EXERCISE 23: Complete the sentences. Use the SIMPLE PAST or the PAST PROGRESSIVE.

1. I *(have)* _____ a busy day yesterday. I *(go)* _____ to

   class in the morning. I *(eat)* _____ lunch with my brother after class.

   In the afternoon, I *(drive)* _____ to the airport to pick up my cousin. I

   (take) _____ her to a restaurant for dinner. After dinner, we *(go)*

   _____ back to my apartment and *(watch)* _____ a

   movie on TV. After the movie, we *(talk)* _____ for a couple of

   hours before we *(go)* _____ to bed.

2. While I *(walk)* _____ to class yesterday morning, I *(see)*

   _____ Abdullah. We *(say)* _____ hello and *(walk)*

   _____ the rest of the way to school together.

3. I *(eat)* _____ lunch with my brother when I suddenly

   (remember) _____ my promise to pick my cousin up at
   the airport.

4. While I *(drive)* _____ to the airport, I *(see)* _____
   an accident.

5. While my cousin and I *(have)* _____ dinner at the

   restaurant last night, we *(see)* _____ a friend of mine. I *(introduce)*

   _____ her to my cousin.

6. When I *(hear)* _____ a knock at the door last night, I *(walk)*

   _____ to the door and *(open)* _____ it.

7. When I *(open)* _____ the door, I *(see)* _____ my brother. I

   (greet) _____ him and *(ask)* _____ him to come in.

8. My cousin and I *(watch)* _____ a movie on TV

   last night when my brother *(come)* _____. He *(watch)*

   _____ the end of the movie with us.

■ **EXERCISE 24:**   Complete the sentences. Use the SIMPLE PAST or the PAST PROGRESSIVE.

1. Mrs. Reed *(turn)* _____ on the radio in her car while she *(drive)*

_____ home yesterday. She *(listen)* _____

to some music when she suddenly *(hear)* _____ a siren.

When she *(look)* _____ in her rearview mirror, she *(see)* _____

an ambulance behind her. She immediately *(pull)* _____ her car

to the side of the road and *(wait)* _____ for the ambulance to pass.

2. I *(have)* _____ a strange experience yesterday. I *(read)*

_____ my book on the bus when a man *(sit)*

_____ down next to me and *(hand)* _____ me some

money. I *(want, not)* _____ his money. I *(be)*

_____ very confused. I *(stand)* _____ up and

(walk) _____ toward the door of the bus. While I *(wait)*

_____ for the door to open, the man *(offer)*

_____ me some money again. When the door *(open)*

_____, I *(get)* _____ off the bus quickly. I still don't

know why he was trying to give me money.

3. A: I *(be)* _____ at my friends' house last night. While we *(eat)*

_____ dinner, their cat *(jump)* _____

on the table. My friends *(seem, not)* _____

_____ to care, but I lost my appetite.

B: What *(you, say)* _____ ?
A: Nothing.

B: Why *(you, ask, not)* _____ your friends to get their cat off the table?

A: I *(want, not)* _____ to be impolite.
B: I think your friends were impolite to let their cat sit on the table during dinner.

■ **EXERCISE 25—REVIEW:** Choose the best completion.

1. I was watching TV. I heard a knock on the door. When I heard the knock on the

door, I _____ it.
    A. open   C. opened
    B. am opening   D. was opening

2. "When _____ you talk to Jane?"
   "Yesterday."
    A. do   B. should   C. did   D. were

3. I _____ TV when Gina called last night. We talked for an hour.
    A. watch   C. was watching
    B. watched   D. am watching

4. Mike is in his bedroom right now. He _____, so we need to be quiet.
   A. is sleeping   C. slept
   B. sleeps   D. was sleeping

5. Kate _____ tell us the truth yesterday. She lied to us.
   A. don't   B. doesn't   C. didn't   D. wasn't

6. I saw a fish while I _____ in the ocean yesterday.
   A. swim   C. were swimming
   B. was swimming   D. was swimming

7. When I heard the phone ring, I _____ it.
   A. answer   C. answered
   B. am answering   D. was answering

8. "_____ you go to concerts often?"
   "Yes. I go at least once a month."
   A. Do   B. Did   C. Was   D. Were

9. While I _____ dinner last night, I burned my finger.
   A. cooking   B. cook   C. was cooking   D. was cook

10. "Where _____ after work yesterday?"
    A. you went   B. you did go   C. did you went   D. did you go

10-11 USING *HAVE BEEN* (THE PRESENT PERFECT)

SITUATION: I came to this city on February 1st. It is now April 1st. I am still in this city. (a) I *have been* here *since February 1st.* (b) I *have been* here *for* two months. SITUATION: Kim came to this city on January 1st. It is now April 1st. Kim is still in this city. (c) Kim *has been* here *since January.* (d) Kim *has been* here *for* three months.	*Have been* expresses the idea that a situation began in the past and still exists at present. *Have been* is used with *since* or *for* to tell how long the situation has existed. (a) and (b) have the same meaning. Third person singular = *has been*, as in (c) and (d).

SITUATION: I came to the classroom at nine o'clock. I am in the classroom now. It's nine-thirty now.
(e) I *have been* here *since nine o'clock.*
(f) I *have been* here *for 30 minutes.*
 	
SITUATION: Ann lives in another city. She came to visit me Monday morning. Now it is Friday morning. She is still here.
(g) Ann *has been* here *since Monday.*
(h) Ann *has been* here *for four days.*
	Since is followed by *a specific time*:
	    since February (specific month)
	    since nine o'clock (specific clock time)
	    since 1995 (specific year)
	
	For is followed by *a length of time*:
	    for two months (number of months)
	    for 30 minutes (length of clock time)
	    for four days (number of days)
	    for three years (number of years)

■ **EXERCISE 26:** Complete the sentences with *since* or *for*.

1. I came to this city six months ago. I am still here. I have been in this city

    _____*for*_____ six months.

2. Kim has been in this city _____*since*_____ January.

3. It's now two o'clock. Carmen has been in class _____*since*_____ one o'clock.

4. Carmen has been in class _____*for*_____ an hour.

5. Erica has been a teacher _____*since*_____ 1994.

6. Mr. Gow has been a plumber _____*for*_____ 20 years.

7. My parents are visiting me this week. They have been here _____*for*_____ five days.

8. They have been here _____*since*_____ last Saturday.

9. India has been an independent nation _____*since*_____ 1947.

10. I have been awake _____*since*_____ six o'clock this morning.

11. My friend is very ill. She has been in the hospital _____*for*_____ four days.

12. I hope the weather gets warmer soon. It's been cold and rainy _____*for*_____ two weeks.

■ **EXERCISE 27:** Complete the following with your own words.

Example:

a. Today is _____*Monday, March 4*_____.

b. I came to this city _____*in January* OR: *two months*_____.

c. I have been in this city since _____*January*_____.

d. I have been in this city for _____*two months*_____.

Example:

a. Today is _____*Monday, March 4*_____.

b. I came to this city _____*on Friday, March 1* OR: *three days*_____.

c. I have been in this city since _____*Friday* OR: *March 1*_____.

d. I have been in this city for _____*three days*_____.

1. a. Today is _Jun 14, 00_.

   b. I came to this city _one yer ago / in Jun, 1999_,

   c. I have been in this city since _Jun, 1999_.

   d. I have been in this city for _a year_.

2. a. Today is _Jun 14, 00_.

   b. _G-an_____* came to this city _two years ago_.

   c. _He_____ has been in this city since _1998_.

   d. _He_____ has been in this city for _two years_.

3. a. I am in the classroom. The time right now is _10 o'clock_.

   b. The time I entered the classroom today was _9 o'clock_.

   c. I have been in this room since _9 o'clock_.

   d. I have been in this room for _an hour_.

4. a. Our teacher taught her/his first class in her/his life _in 1974_.

   b. She/He has been a teacher since _1974_.

   c. She/He has been a teacher for _26 years_.

5. a. I started to go to school in (year) _1998_. I am still a student.

   b. I have been a student since _1996_.

   c. I have been a student for _four yers_.

10-12 USING *SINCE*-CLAUSES

(a)	I've been afraid of dogs | since I was a child. main clause since-clause	**Since** can be followed by a subject and verb. In (a): *since I was child* = a *since*-clause.*
(b)	Mr. Lo has been a teacher **since** he graduated from college.	Notice in the examples: The verb in the main clause is **present perfect**. The verb in the *since*-clause is **simple past**.
(c)	Sue and I have been friends **since** we were children.	

In (a) above the since-clause is labeled: S V over *since I was a child.*

*A *since*-clause is a time clause. See Charts 5-18 and 5-19 for more information about time clauses.

_____

*Use the name of a classmate.

■ **EXERCISE 28:** Complete the sentences with the words in parentheses. Use the PRESENT PERFECT or the SIMPLE PAST.

1. Maria got some bad news last week. She *(be)* ___has been___ sad since she *(get)* ___got___ the bad news.

2. I started school when I was five years old. I *(be)* ___have been___ in school since I *(be)* ___was___ five years old.

3. Ann's brother arrived a few days ago to visit her. She loves her brother and is happy to be with him. She *(be)* ___has been___ happy since her brother *(come)* ___came___.

4. Jack moved to Hong Kong after he graduated from the university. Jim *(be)* ___has been___ in Hong Kong since he *(graduate)* ___graduated___ from the university.

5. The weather was hot and dry for many weeks. Two days ago it rained. The weather *(be)* ___has been___ cool and wet since it *(rain)* ___rained___ two days ago.

6. Jack broke his leg five days ago. He's in the hospital. He *(be)* ___has been___ in the hospital since he *(break)* ___broke___ his leg.

SIMPLE FORM	SIMPLE PAST	PAST PARTICIPLE	
be	was, were	**been**	Form of the present perfect: **have/has** + past participle
know	knew	**known**	Irregular verbs have irregular past participles. (See Chart 10-18 and Appendix 5 for additional lists of irregular verbs.)
have	had	**had**	
see	saw	**seen**	
teach	taught	**taught**	
live	lived	**lived**	The past participle of regular verbs is the same form as the simple past: verb + **-ed**
own	owned	**owned**	
work	worked	**worked**	
touch	touched	**touched**	

(a) I **have known** Tom for five years. (b) Sue **has had** a bad cold for three days. (c) They **have lived** here since 1994. (d) We **have owned** our own home since 1989.	Notice in the examples: The present perfect is formed by **have / has** + past participle.
(e) I've We've You've They've } been here for two months. She's He's It's	**Have** and **has** are contracted with *subject pronouns* as shown in the examples.
COMPARE (f) **She's** been here for two months. (g) **She's** in my class.	In (f): *she's = she has* In (g): *she's = she is*

■ **EXERCISE 29:** Complete the sentences with the given verbs. Use the PRESENT PERFECT.

1. *teach*   Mr. Jackson is a teacher. He _____'s taught_____ biology for twenty years.

2. *know*   I _____ Mary Adams since I was a child.

3. *be*   She _____ a good friend for a long time.

4. *live*   My parents live in a suburb of Mexico City. They _____ _____ in the same apartment for twenty-five years.

5. *have*   Janet and Sam _____ their dog Fido for three years.

6. *work*   My uncle _____ at the automobile factory for seventeen years.

7. *be*   We _____ in class since nine o'clock this morning.

8. *own*   Ken is a businessman. He sells car parts. He _____ his own business since 1994.

9. *have*   Mr. Cook's hair started to turn gray when he was forty. He _____ _____ gray hair since he was forty years old.

10. *see*   I _____ several movies since I came to this city.

■ **EXERCISE 30—ORAL:** Complete the sentences with the given verbs and your own words. Use the PRESENT PERFECT.

    Example: know   I . . . *(name of a person)* for . . . .
              →   *I've known Li Ming for three months.*
              →   *My best friend is Maria Alvarez. I've known her for fifteen years.*

    1. *be*   I . . . in this classroom today since . . . .
    2. *live*   Right now I am living *(in an apartment, a dorm, etc.)*. I . . . there since . . . .
    3. *have*   I have *(name of something you own)*. I . . . it/them for . . . .
    4. *be*   I . . . in *(name of a place)* since . . . .
    5. *know*   I . . . *(name of a classmate)* since . . . .
    6. *work*   *(name of someone you know)* works at *(name of a place)*. He/She . . . there for . . . .
    7. *be*   I . . . awake since . . . .
    8. *teach*   Our teacher . . . English since . . . .
    9. *live*   My *(name of a family member)* . . . *(name of a place)* for . . . .
   10. *be*   I . . . afraid of . . . since . . . .

10-14   USING *NEVER* WITH THE PRESENT PERFECT

(a) *I've **never** touched an elephant.* (b) Anna *has **never** seen* the Pacific Ocean.	***Never*** is frequently used with the *present perfect*. In (a): the speaker is saying, "From the beginning of my life to the present moment, I have never touched an elephant. In my entire lifetime, since I was born, I have never touched an elephant."

■ **EXERCISE 31—ORAL:** Use *never* with the PRESENT PERFECT.

    Example: Name some places you have never lived.
    STUDENT A: I've never lived in a small town.
    STUDENT B: I've never lived in a dormitory.
    STUDENT C: I've never lived in South America.
    STUDENT D: Etc.

    1. countries you've never been in   4. animals you've never touched
    2. cities you've never lived in   5. things you've never seen
    3. pets you've never had   6. things you've never owned

10-15 PRESENT PERFECT: QUESTIONS AND NEGATIVES

(a) **Have** *you* **lived** here for a long time? (b) **Has** *Ken* **been** in this class since the beginning of the term?	Question form of the present perfect: **have/has** + *subject* + *past participle*
(c) I **have not (haven't) lived** here for a long time. (d) Ken **has not (hasn't) been** in the class since the beginning of the term.	Negative form of the present perfect: **have/has** + **not** + *past participle* Negative contractions: *have not = haven't* *has not = hasn't*

■ **EXERCISE 32:** Complete the sentences with the PRESENT PERFECT.

1. *(Mr. Jackson, teach)* _____*Has Mr. Jackson taught*_____ biology for a long time?

2. Ms. Smith is a new teacher. She *(teach, not)* _____*hasn't taught*_____ biology for a long time.

3. *(you, know)* _____ Mary Adams since you were a child?

4. I met Mary Adams only two months ago. I *(know, not)* _____

   _____ her for a long time. I've known her for only a short time.

5. *(she, be)* _____ a good friend of yours for a long time?

6. She *(be, not)* _____ a friend of mine for a long time.

7. *(your parents, live)* _____ near Mexico City for a long time?

8. I came here only a couple of months ago. I *(live, not)* _____ here for a long time.

9. *(Janet and Sam, have)* _____ their dog Fido for a long time?

10. Pedro got his new bicycle a few months ago. He *(have, not)* _____

    _____ his bicycle for a long time.

11. *(your uncle, work)* _____ at the automobile factory for a long time?

12. My aunt has a new job at a candy factory. She *(work, not)* _____ there for a long time.

450 ■ CHAPTER 10

10-16 USING *EVER* WITH THE PRESENT PERFECT

(a) *Have* you **ever** *been* in Hawaii? (b) *Has* Pedro **ever** *had* a job (in his lifetime)?	In (a): **ever** means "in your lifetime, from the time you were born to the present moment." Questions with **ever** frequently use the present perfect.

(c) A: Have you ever been in London?
    B: Yes, I **have**. (I have been in London.)
(d) A: Has Tom ever lived in Chicago?
    B: Yes, he **has**. (He has lived in Chicago.)
(e) A: Have you ever been in Korea?
    B: No, I **haven't**. (I haven't ever been in Korea.)
(f) A: Has Sue ever lived in Paris?
    B: No, she **hasn't**. (She hasn't ever lived in Paris.)
	In a short answer to a yes/no question with the present perfect, the helping verb (**have** or **has**) is used.
	In (c): Speaker B is saying that he has been in London at some time in his lifetime.

(g) I **haven't ever been** in Korea.
(h) I**'ve never been** in Korea.
(i) She **hasn't ever lived** in Paris.
(j) She**'s never lived** in Paris.
	(g) and (h) have the same meaning.
	    haven't ever been = have never been
	(i) and (j) have the same meaning.
	    hasn't ever lived = has never lived

■ **EXERCISE 33:** Answer the questions. Use short answers.

1. A: *(you, be, ever)* _____Have you ever been_____ in Russia?

   B: No, I _____haven't_____. I *(be, never)* _____'ve never been_____ in Russia.

2. A: *(you, be, ever)* _____ in Turkey?

   B: Yes, I _____. I *(be)* _____ in Turkey several times.

3. A: *(you, visit, ever)* _____ the
   Metropolitan Museum of Art in New York City?

   B: No, I _____. I *(visit, never)* _____
   that museum.

4. A: *(Sam, be, ever)* _____ in Argentina?

   B: No, he _____. He *(be, never)* _____
   in Argentina.

5. A: *(Carmen, be, ever)* _____ in Canada?

   B: Yes, she _____. She *(be)* _____ there many times.

6. A: *(you, have, ever)* _____ a serious illness?

   B: No, I _____. I *(have, never)* _____
      a serious illness. I've been very lucky.

7. A: *(your brother, live, ever)* _____
      in an apartment by himself?

   B: No, he _____. He still lives with my parents.

8. A: *(you, talk, ever)* _____ to a famous
      person?

   B: No, I _____. I don't know any famous people.

9. A: *(you, see, ever)* _____

      _____ a hummingbird?

   B: Yes, I _____.

■ **EXERCISE 34—ORAL (BOOKS CLOSED):**   Answer the questions. Use short answers.
      Several people should answer the same question.

      Example: Have you ever been in (Africa)?
      STUDENT A: No, I haven't.
      STUDENT B: No, I haven't.
      STUDENT C: Yes, I have.

      1. Have you ever been in (Egypt)? (Italy)?
      2. Have you ever been to (Indonesia)? (Venezuela)?★
      3. Have you ever been in (Washington, D.C.)? (Tokyo)?
      4. Have you ever been to (Toronto)? (Istanbul)?
      5. Have you ever had a pet?
      6. Have you ever had a bicycle?
      7. Have you ever had a *(kind of car)*?
      8. Have you ever had a purple umbrella?
      9. Have you ever lived in an apartment? a dormitory?
     10. Have you ever lived in a one-room apartment?
     11. Have you ever lived in *(name of a city or country)*?
     12. Have you ever touched an elephant? a snake? a cow?
     13. Have you ever called (. . .) on the phone?
     14. Have you ever stayed in a hotel in this city?
     15. Have you ever watched *(name of a program)* on TV?
     16. Have you ever been to *(name of a place in this city)*?
     17. Have you ever seen a whale?

      _____
      ★*Have you ever been in Indonesia* and *Have you ever been to Indonesia* have the same meaning.

10-17 THE PRESENT PERFECT: QUESTIONS WITH *HOW LONG*

(a) A: *How long **have** you **been*** in this city? B: For five months. (b) A: *How long **has** Ali **had*** a mustache? B: Since he was twenty-one years old. (c) A: *How long **have** you **known*** Maria? B: Since the beginning of the school term.	Question form of the present perfect: ***have*** + *subject* + *past participle*

■ **EXERCISE 35:** Complete the sentences with the words in parentheses.

1. A: How long *(you, be)* _____*have you been*_____ at this school?
    B: Since the middle of January.

2. A: How long *(you, know)* _____ Shelley?
    B: For three years.

3. A: How long *(Mr. Lake, be)* _____ a teacher?
    B: Since he graduated from college in 1990.

4. A: How long *(you, have)* _____ your car?
    B: For a couple of years.

5. A: How long *(your roommate, be)* _____
    out of town?
    B: Since Friday.

■ **EXERCISE 36—ORAL:** Pair up with a classmate.

PART I:
STUDENT A: Ask questions with ***how long*** and the PRESENT PERFECT.
STUDENT B: Answer the questions.

Example: have a mustache
STUDENT A: How long have you had a mustache?
STUDENT B: I've had a mustache since I was seventeen years old.

1. be in *(this city/country)*
2. be in this class
3. know *(name of a classmate)*
4. be a student at *(this school)*
5. be in this room today
6. live at your present address
7. have *(something Student B owns)*
8. have *(something else Student B owns)*

PART II: *Switch roles.*

STUDENT A: Ask the questions. If the answer is yes, ask for more information, including **how long**. Use the PRESENT PERFECT in the question with **how long**. If the answer is no, think of other similar questions until Student B answers yes.

STUDENT B: Answer the questions.

Example: Do you have a pet?

STUDENT A: Do you have a pet?

STUDENT B: Yes, I do.

STUDENT A: What kind of pet do you have?

STUDENT B: A dog.

STUDENT A: How long have you had your dog?

STUDENT B: She's six years old. I've had her since she was a puppy. I've had her for six years.

Example: Do you have a pet?

STUDENT A: Do you have a pet?

STUDENT B: No.

STUDENT A: Do your parents have a pet?

STUDENT B: No.

STUDENT A: Does anyone you know have a pet?

STUDENT B: Yes. My brother does.

STUDENT A: What kind of pet does he have?

STUDENT B: A cat.

STUDENT A: How long has he had a cat?

STUDENT B: For five or six years.

9. Do you have a pet? (Do your parents? Does anyone you know have a pet?)

10. Are you a student at *(this school)?*

11. Do you live in an apartment? (a dormitory? a house?)

12. Do you have a roommate?

13. Do you have a briefcase or a bookbag? (a wallet? a purse?)

14. Do you know *(name of a classmate)?*

15. Do you have a car? (a bicycle? a personal computer? a calculator?)

16. Are you married? (Is the teacher married? Is anyone in this class married?)

(a) I *have* never ***touched*** an elephant.	The past participles of regular verbs end in ***-ed***.
(b) *Has* Jim ever ***stayed*** at a hotel in Bangkok?	Examples: *touched, stayed*.
(c) Tom *has* never ***eaten*** Thai food.	Irregular verbs have *irregular* past participles.
(d) *Have* you ever ***gone*** to a rock concert?	Examples: *eaten, gone*.

THE PRINCIPAL PARTS OF SOME COMMON IRREGULAR VERBS

Simple Form	Simple Past	Past Participle
be	*was, were*	*been*
eat	*ate*	*eaten*
go	*went*	*gone*
have	*had*	*had*
know	*knew*	*known*
lose	*lost*	*lost*
meet	*met*	*met*
read	*read★*	*read★*
see	*saw*	*seen*
speak	*spoke*	*spoken*
take	*took*	*taken*
teach	*taught*	*taught*
tell	*told*	*told*
wear	*wore*	*worn*
write	*wrote*	*written*

★ The simple past and the past participle of the verb ***read*** are both pronounced "red" — the same pronunciation as the color red.

■ **EXERCISE 37—ORAL (BOOKS CLOSED):** Add the PAST PARTICIPLE.

Example: eat, ate, . . .
Response: eaten

1. eat, ate, . . .
2. go, went, . . .
3. have, had, . . .
4. know, knew, . . .
5. lose, lost, . . .
6. meet, met, . . .
7. read, read, . . .
8. see, saw, . . .
9. speak, spoke, . . .
10. take, took, . . .
11. tell, told, . . .
12. wear, wore, . . .
13. write, wrote, . . .

■ **EXERCISE 38:** Complete the sentences with the correct form of the words in the list.

PART I:

go	✔ *take*
lose	*tell*
meet	*write*

1. I've never _____*taken*_____ a physics class.

2. Have you ever _____ Maria's sister?

3. Have you ever _____ the keys to your apartment?

4. I've never _____ to a rock concert in my whole life.

5. Have you ever _____ a lie?

6. Have you ever _____ a poem?

PART II:

eat	*see*
know	*speak*
read	*wear*

7. How long have you _____ Abdul? Have you been friends for a long time?

8. I've never _____ the movie *Gone with the Wind*.

9. Have you ever _____ the book *Gone with the Wind?*

10. Ann has never _____ raw meat.

11. Mr. Cook never dresses casually. He has never _____ blue jeans in his life.

12. Have you ever _____ to your teacher on the phone?

■ **EXERCISE 39—ORAL:** Pair up with a classmate.

STUDENT A: Your book is open. Ask a question beginning with *"Have you ever . . . ?"*
STUDENT B: Your book is closed. Give a short answer to the question.

Example: be in *(name of a country)*
STUDENT A: Have you ever been in Malaysia?
STUDENT B: Yes, I have. OR: No, I haven't.

1. meet *(name of a person)*
2. go to *(a place in this city)*
3. lose the keys to your front door
4. be in *(name of a building in this city)*
5. read *(name of a book)*
6. wear cowboy boots
7. speak to *(name of a classmate)* about *(something)*
8. eat fish eggs
9. write a letter to *(name of a person)*
10. tell *(name of the teacher)* about *(something)*
11. see *(name of a movie)*
12. have *(name of a kind of food)*

Switch roles.
13. read *(name of a book)*
14. eat *(a kind of food)*
15. write a letter to *(name of a person)*
16. see *(name of a television program)*
17. go to *(a place in this city)*
18. have *(name of a kind of food)*
19. be in *(name of a place at this school)*
20. meet *(name of a person)*
21. wear *(a kind of clothing)*
22. speak to *(name of a teacher)* about *(something)*
23. lose *(name of something Student B has)*
24. tell *(name of a classmate)* about *(something)*

■ **EXERCISE 40—ERROR ANALYSIS:** Find and correct the mistakes.

1. Let's going to a restaurant for dinner tonight.

2. I've never see a whale.

3. The phone rang while I was eat dinner last night.

4. How long you have been a student at this school?

5. Ken doesn't has to go to work today.

6. I must to study tonight. I can't going to the movie with you.

7. I have been in this city since two months.

8. Why you have to leave now?

9. You shouldn't to speak loudly in a library.

10. I've known Olga since I am a child.

11. You don't must be late for work.

12. Have you ever went to a baseball game?

13. I am in this class since the beginning of January.

■ **EXERCISE 41—WRITTEN:** Write about your experiences as a member of this class.
Suggestions of things to write about:
   • the first day of class
   • the teacher
   • your classmates
   • the classroom
   • your learning experiences
   • the textbook(s)
   • a memorable event in this class

The English Alphabet

A	a		N	n
B	b		O	o
C	c		P	p
D	d		Q	q
E	e		R	r
F	f		S	s
G	g		T	t
H	h		U	u
I	i		V	v
J	j		W	w
K	k		X	x
L	l		Y	y
M	m		Z	z★

Vowels = *a, e, i, o u.*
Consonants = *b, c, d, f, g, h, j, k, l, m, n, p, q, r, s, t, v, w, x, y, z.*

★The letter "z" is pronounced "zee" in American English and "zed" in British English.

APPENDIX 2
Numbers

1	one	1st	first
2	two	2nd	second
3	three	3rd	third
4	four	4th	fourth
5	five	5th	fifth
6	six	6th	sixth
7	seven	7th	seventh
8	eight	8th	eighth
9	nine	9th	ninth
10	ten	10th	tenth
11	eleven	11th	eleventh
12	twelve	12th	twelfth
13	thirteen	13th	thirteenth
14	fourteen	14th	fourteenth
15	fifteen	15th	fifteenth
16	sixteen	16th	sixteenth
17	seventeen	17th	seventeenth
18	eighteen	18th	eighteenth
19	nineteen	19th	nineteenth
20	twenty	20th	twentieth
21	twenty-one	21th	twenty-first
22	twenty-two	22nd	twenty-second
23	twenty-three	23rd	twenty-third
24	twenty-four	24th	twenty-fourth
25	twenty-five	25th	twenty-fifth
26	twenty-six	26th	twenty-sixth
27	twenty-seven	27th	twenty-seventh
28	twenty-eight	28th	twenty-eighth
29	twenty-nine	29th	twenty-ninth
30	thirty	30th	thirtieth
40	forty	40th	fortieth
50	fifty	50th	fiftieth
60	sixty	60th	sixtieth
70	seventy	70th	seventieth
80	eighty	80th	eightieth
90	ninety	90th	ninetieth
100	one hundred	100th	one hundredth
200	two hundred	200th	two hundredth
1,000	one thousand		
10,000	ten thousand		
100,000	one hundred thousand		
1,000,000	one million		

Days of the Week and Months of the Year

DAYS

Monday	(Mon.)
Tuesday	(Tues.)
Wednesday	(Wed.)
Thursday	(Thurs.)
Friday	(Fri.)
Saturday	(Sat.)
Sunday	(Sun.)

MONTHS

January	(Jan.)
February	(Feb.)
March	(Mar.)
April	(Apr.)
May	(May)
June	(June)
July	(July)
August	(Aug.)
September	(Sept.)
October	(Oct.)
November	(Nov.)
December	(Dec.)

Using numbers to write the date:

month/day/year
10/31/41 = October 31, 1941
4/15/92 = April 15, 1992

Saying dates:

USUAL WRITTEN FORM	USUAL SPOKEN FORM
January 1	January first/the first of January
March 2	March second/the second of March
May 3	May third/the third of May
June 4	June fourth/the fourth of June
August 5	August fifth/the fifth of August
October 10	October tenth/the tenth of October
November 27	November twenty-seventh/the twenty-seventh of November

APPENDIX 4
Ways of Saying the Time

9:00	It's nine o'clock.
	It's nine.
9:05	It's nine-oh-five.
	It's five (minutes) after nine.
	It's five (minutes) past nine.
9:10	It's nine-ten.
	It's ten (minutes) after nine.
	It's ten (minutes) past nine.
9:15	It's nine-fifteen.
	It's a quarter after nine.
	It's a quarter past nine.
9:30	It's nine-thirty.
	It's half past nine.
9:45	It's nine-forty-five.
	It's a quarter to ten.
	It's a quarter of ten.
9:50	It's nine-fifty.
	It's ten (minutes) to ten.
	It's ten (minutes) of ten.
12:00	It's noon.
	It's midnight.

A.M. = morning   It's nine A.M.
P.M. = afternoon/evening/night   It's nine P.M.

APPENDIX 5

Irregular Verbs

SIMPLE FORM	SIMPLE PAST	PAST PARTICIPLE	SIMPLE FORM	SIMPLE PAST	PAST PARTICIPLE
be	was, were	been	keep	kept	kept
become	became	become	know	knew	known
begin	began	begun	lend	lent	lent
bend	bent	bent	leave	left	left
bite	bit	bitten	lose	lost	lost
blow	blew	blown	make	made	made
break	broke	broken	meet	met	met
bring	brought	brought	pay	paid	paid
build	built	built	put	put	put
buy	bought	bought	read	read	read
catch	caught	caught	ride	rode	ridden
choose	chose	chosen	ring	rang	rung
come	came	come	run	ran	run
cost	cost	cost	say	said	said
cut	cut	cut	see	saw	seen
do	did	done	sell	sold	sold
draw	drew	drawn	send	sent	sent
drink	drank	drunk	shake	shook	shaken
drive	drove	driven	shut	shut	shut
eat	ate	eaten	sing	sang	sung
fall	fell	fallen	sit	sat	sat
feed	fed	fed	sleep	slept	slept
feel	felt	felt	speak	spoke	spoken
fight	fought	fought	spend	spent	spent
find	found	found	stand	stood	stood
fly	flew	flown	steal	stole	stolen
forget	forgot	forgotten	swim	swam	swum
get	got	gotten/got	take	took	taken
give	gave	given	teach	taught	taught
go	went	gone	tear	tore	torn
grow	grew	grown	tell	told	told
hang	hung	hung	think	thought	thought
have	had	had	throw	threw	thrown
hear	heard	heard	understand	understood	understood
hide	hid	hidden	wake up	woke up	woken up
hit	hit	hit	wear	wore	worn
hold	held	held	win	won	won
hurt	hurt	hurt	write	wrote	written

Index